At Issue

Is Media Violence
a Problem?

Other Books in the At Issue Series:

At Issue

Is Media Violence a Problem?

David M. Haugen, Book Editor

GREENHAVEN PRESS

An imprint of Thomson Gale, a part of The Thomson Corporation

Detroit • New York • San Francisco • New Haven, Conn. • Waterville, Maine • London

Christine Nasso, *Publisher*
Elizabeth Des Chenes, *Managing Editor*

© 2007 Thomson Gale, a part of The Thomson Corporation.

Thomson and Star logo are trademarks and Gale and Greenhaven Press are registered trademarks used herein under license.

For more information, contact:
Greenhaven Press
27500 Drake Rd.
Farmington Hills, MI 48331-3535
Or you can visit our Internet site at http://www.gale.com

LIBRARY OF CONGRESS CATALOGING-IN-PUBLICATION DATA

Is media violence a problem? / David M. Haugen, book editor.
    p. cm. -- (At issue)
  Includes bibliographical references and index.
  ISBN-13: 978-0-7377-2398-4 (lib. : alk. paper)
  ISBN-10: 0-7377-2398-X (lib. : alk. paper)
  ISBN-13: 978-0-7377-2399-1 (pbk. : alk. paper)
  ISBN-10: 0-7377-2399-8 (pbk. : alk. paper)
  1. Mass media and children. 2. Mass media and teenagers. 3. Violence in mass media. 4. Children and violence. I. Haugen, David M., 1969–
  HQ784.M3I8 2007
  303.6083--dc22
                                        2006024682

Printed in the United States of America
10 9 8 7 6 5 4 3 2 1

Contents

Introduction

On June 7, 2003, eighteen-year-old Devin Moore was brought into a police station in Fayetteville, Alabama, under suspicion that he had stolen a car. At the station he cooperated during the booking process then, without warning, he snapped. Moore attacked the arresting officer, took his .40-caliber automatic pistol and shot him twice, killing him. Moore exited the room and proceeded down the hallway of the station. There, he met another officer who was on his way to investigate the shots. Moore fired the weapon and hit the officer three times. Before leaving the station, the young man grabbed the keys to a police car waiting outside and found one more victim in the emergency dispatcher. He shot this man five times, with one fatal bullet landing in the head. Moore drove off in the police car, leaving the carnage behind. The entire episode played out in less than sixty seconds.

Moore had no history of criminal activity or violence, prompting many to question what had caused such an unprovoked and violent outburst. For the families of the murder victims, however, the answer was quite clear. In March 2006, they filed a multimillion-dollar lawsuit, claiming that the influence of the video game *Grand Theft Auto: Vice City*, prompted Devin Moore to kill. As investigations into the incident began, it was learned that Moore played the video game often in the months leading up to the murders; one scenario in the game even bears stunning resemblance to what happened that day in June. Moore's lawyers also cited the video game influence as the motivating factor in the murders, hoping to show that Moore was not thinking clearly when he committed the heinous acts. They referred to a statement Moore had made after being captured: "Life is like a video game. Everybody's got to die sometime."

The tie between video game violence and real-life crime reaches beyond this incident. Detectives in Oakland, California, cited *Grand Theft Auto III*, another game in the popular series, as the catalyst for the seemingly random crimes, including six homicides, committed by a gang of six individuals in 2003. Also in 2003, two teenagers claimed this same game was the main influence that prompted them to fire a .22-caliber rifle at passing cars on the highway in Newport, Tennessee. This sniping ended with the death of one person. In light of these events, many critics argued that the new breed of realistic and hyper-violent video games was an undeniable catalyst for real-world mayhem and murder.

The connection between violent behavior and the media, however, dates back to a time long before video games. In the 1950s comic books were among the first media to be singled out as a force contributing to juvenile delinquency. Since then, the focus has shifted toward television, music, movies, and most recently video games. Numerous studies have been conducted in an effort to identify and understand if there is a connection between increased exposure to media violence and the occurrence of violent crimes. One group that has focused attention on this subject is the American Psychological Association (APA). In 2006 the APA reported that, "Extensive research has shown that higher levels of children's exposure to media violence correlate with increased acceptance of aggressive attitudes and increased aggressive behavior. Recent studies associate exposure to violence in the media with violent behaviors."

Even with this strong statement the APA only asserts that there may be a correlation and association between media violence and violent acts. It has been careful not to claim that there is a causal link between the two. Professor Jonathan Freedman from the University of Toronto stated in 1996, "Correlations do not prove causality. Boys watch more TV football than girls, and they play more football than girls, but no one, so far as I know, believes that television is what makes boys more interested in football." Freedman has continued his research into studies on media violence and published the book *Media Violence and Its Effect on Aggression: Assessing the Scientific Evidence* in 2002. He maintains that fewer than half of approximately 200 studies conducted proved that violence in the media caused real violence.

Many individuals argue that in addition to the stimulus of violent media, other influential factors must be considered. Education, social and economic background, and a predisposition toward violent behavior are all raised as important considerations when examining the causes of violence. Kevin Durkin, an associate professor of psychology at the University of Western Australia, implicates parents as a causal factor, stating, "High television [viewing] is correlated with lax parenting; aggressive behavior in children is also correlated with lax parenting; hence, it is possible that the real source of the problem is family management."

While some observers focus on the negative repercussions of violent media, others suggest that it may have cathartic qualities. Media's defenders insist that instead of inducing violence, video games and other venues for aggression allow individuals to reduce their anger by engaging with it in a fantasy world. Psychologist Melanie Moore states, "Children need violent entertainment in order to explore the inescapable feelings that they've been taught to deny, and to reintegrate those feelings into a more whole, more complex, more resilient selfhood." In this light, violent media is an avenue of development, not a detrimental pastime.

As the aforementioned viewpoints illustrate, there is no consensus on how violent media affects individual behavior. Various studies assert positive or negative influences, while other analyses suggest there may be no connection at all. The United States courts, however, came to a more definitive conclusion in the case of Devin Moore. On August 9, 2005, the then-twenty-year-old young man was found guilty of murder in an Alabama court. The jury did not find the video game *Grand Theft Auto: Vice City* to blame, and Moore was sentenced to death for his crime. No U.S. court has yet to endorse a causal relationship between media violence and real-life violence.

The authors in Greenhaven Press's *At Issue: Is Media Violence a Problem?* examine the phenomenon and influence of media violence from a variety of perspectives. They look at various forms of media, including television, music, movies, and video games, and debate the impact of these upon individuals and society as a whole. Although some of these critics and analysts have definite views upon the influence of violent media, it is evident from the diversity of opinions that the debate will continue as long as media remains central to American culture.

Media Violence Contributes to a More Violent Society

Craig A. Anderson and Brad J. Bushman

Craig A. Anderson is a professor of psychology at Iowa State University in Ames, Iowa. Brad J. Bushman was Anderson's colleague at Ames but now teaches psychology at the University of Michigan in Ann Arbor. Both have written extensively on media violence and its influence on society.

Numerous studies spanning many years and involving thousands of participants clearly show that media violence is causally linked to increased aggression in individuals. Despite the overwhelming evidence, the public is still swayed by media reports that downplay the connection. Intervention at a young age will be needed to reduce the impact of media violence and thus decrease the rate of aggressive violence in society.

Concerns about the negative effects of prolonged exposure to violent television programming emerged shortly after broadcasting began in 1946. By 1972 sufficient empirical evidence had accumulated for the U.S. Surgeon General to comment that "... televised violence, indeed, does have an adverse effect on certain members of our society." Other scientific bodies have come to similar conclusions. Six major professional societies in the United States—the American Psychological Association, the American Academy of Pediatrics, the American Academy of Child and Adolescent Psychiatry, the

Craig A. Anderson and Brad J. Bushman, "The Effects of Media Violence on Society," *Science*, vol. 295, March 29, 2002, pp. 2377, 2379. Copyright 2002 by AAAS. Reprinted with permission.

American Medical Association, the American Academy of Family Physicians, and the American Psychiatric Association—... concluded [in 2000] that "the data point overwhelmingly to a causal connection between media violence and aggressive behavior in some children." In a report [from the March 2002 issue of *Science*, J.G.], Johnson and colleagues present important evidence showing that extensive TV viewing among adolescents and young adults is associated with subsequent aggressive acts.

The Causal Link Has Been Established

Despite the consensus among experts, lay people do not seem to be getting the message from the popular press that media violence contributes to a more violent society. We recently demonstrated that even as the scientific evidence linking media violence to aggression has accumulated, news reports about the effects of media violence have shifted to weaker statements, implying that there is little evidence for such effects. This inaccurate reporting in the popular press may account for continuing controversy long after the debate should have been over, much as the cigarette smoking/cancer controversy persisted long after the scientific community knew that smoking causes cancer.

Aggression researchers have adopted a triangulation strategy to examine the effects of violence in the media. Specifically, divergent research methods have been applied in the belief that using several unique methodological approaches yields a clearer picture than would be possible with any single method. Results of a meta-analysis of all available studies investigating the hypothesis that exposure to media violence increases aggression. Experimental studies demonstrate a causal link. Laboratory experiments yield slightly larger effects than other studies, presumably because of greater control over irrelevant factors. Field experiments demonstrate causal effects in naturalistic settings. Cross-sectional studies demonstrate a positive association between media violence and types of real-world aggression (for example, assault) that cannot be studied ethically in experimental settings. Longitudinal studies reveal long-term effects of early media violence exposure on later aggressive acts. These effects are not trivial in magnitude. For example, they are larger than the effects of calcium intake on bone mass or of lead exposure on IQ in children. Interestingly, recent work demonstrates similar-sized effects of violent video games on aggression.

A heavy diet of media violence contributes to a societal violence rate that is unnecessarily obese.

A Significant 2002 Study

The longitudinal study by Johnson and colleagues is important for at least three reasons. It is the first published longitudinal study to link television exposure during adolescence and young adulthood to subsequent aggression, contradicting the common assumption that media violence affects only children. It therefore adds to extant research linking childhood TV habits to adult aggression and violence. Second, its relatively large sample size (707 families) and time span (17 years) allowed a meaningful test of television exposure on severe aggressive behaviors (such as assault and robbery). Third, by statistically controlling for key childhood factors known to affect aggression (including childhood neglect, family income, neighborhood violence, parental education, and psychiatric disorders) the investigators were able to rule out numerous alternative explanations.

One potential problem with the Johnson *et al.* study is the use of hours of TV viewing, rather than hours of viewing violent TV. This is somewhat problematic because the primary source of TV viewing effects on aggression is believed to be violent content. However, about 60% of TV programs contain violence, so the number of TV hours correlates closely with the number of violent TV hours. Thus, the use of TV viewing hours in this study probably underestimates the effects of TV violence.

Recent theory about human aggression suggests at least two approaches to reducing media-related aggression. One involves reducing exposure to violent media. [In 2001 T.N.] Robinson and colleagues reported one such intervention that significantly reduced aggression among third and fourth graders over a 6-month period. The other approach involves changing children's attitudes toward media violence. [In 1983 L.R.] Huesmann successfully used this approach to reduce aggression in first and third graders over a 2-year period. The study by Johnson and colleagues suggests that media violence affects a larger group of people than previously believed, and that interventions for adolescents might also be beneficial. Such approaches are needed because a heavy diet of media violence contributes to a societal violence rate that is unnecessarily obese.

Media Violence Is a Health Risk to Adolescents

American Academy of Pediatrics

The American Academy of Pediatrics (AAP) is an association of 60,000 pediatricians. The AAP aims to disseminate information to improve health care for America's children.

America's children spend many hours a day listening to music or watching movies and television shows laced with violence. They also pass idle moments playing video games in which the players not only experience simulated violence but often perpetrate it. The nation's top medical and psychological institutions agree that this continual exposure to violence has increased aggression in young people. Media violence whether passively absorbed or actively imitated has consequences. Violent crimes, including murder, are rife among America's young, and thousands of children fall victim to youth violence each year. Exposure to media violence is a contributing factor to such real-world tragedies.

At a Congressional Public Health Summit in July 2000, the American Academy of Pediatrics (AAP) was joined by the American Medical Association, the American Academy of Child and Adolescent Psychiatry, and the American Psychological Association in issuing an unprecedented "Joint Statement on the Impact of Entertainment Violence on Children." Although recent school shootings have prompted politicians and the general public to focus their attention on the influence of media violence, the medical community has been con-

American Academy of Pediatrics, "Media Violence," *Pediatrics*, vol. 108, November 2001, pp. 1222–26. Copyright American Academy of Pediatrics. Used with permission.

cerned with this issue since the 1950s. On the basis of a grow-ing and nearly unanimous body of evidence associating media violence with increased aggression in young people, the US Surgeon General issued a special report on the public health effects of media violence in 1972. Ten years later, the National Institute of Mental Health issued a comprehensive review of the research on media violence and its effects, outlining con-cerns for children's psychological health, as did a report gener-ated by the American Psychological Association in 1993.

Exposure to Violent Media

American children between 2 and 18 years of age spend an average of 6 hours and 32 minutes each day using media (television, commercial or self-recorded video, movies, video games, print, radio, recorded music, computer, and the Internet). This is more time than they spend on any other ac-tivity, with the exception of sleeping. When simultaneous use of multiple media is accounted for, that exposure increases to 8 hours a day. A large proportion of this media exposure in-cludes acts of violence that are witnessed or "virtually perpe-trated" (in the form of video games) by young people. It has been estimated that by age 18, the average young person will have viewed 200,000 acts of violence on television alone.

The National Television Violence study evaluated almost 10,000 hours of broadcast programming from 1995 through 1997 and found that 61% of the programming portrayed in-terpersonal violence, much of it in an entertaining or glamor-ized manner. The highest proportion of violence was found in children's shows. Of all animated feature films produced in the United States between 1937 and 1999, 100% portrayed violence, and the amount of violence with intent to injure has increased through the years. More than 80% of the violence portrayed in contemporary music videos is perpetrated by at-tractive protagonists against a disproportionate number of women and blacks. American media, in particular, tend to portray heroes using violence as a justified means of resolving conflict and prevailing over others.

Prolonged exposure to such media portrayals results in increased acceptance of violence as an appropriate means of solving problems and achieving one's goals. Television, movies, and music videos normalize carrying and using weapons and glamorize them as a source of personal power. Children in grades 4 through 8 preferentially choose video games that award points for violence against others. Of the 33 most popular games, 21% feature violence against women. The popular music CD that led the sales charts and swept the Music Television (MTV) Video Music Awards in the year 2000 featured songs about rape and murder with graphic lyrics and sound effects. Because children have high levels of exposure, media have greater access and time to shape young people's attitudes and actions than do parents or teachers, replacing them as educators, role models, and the primary sources of information about the world and how one behaves in it.

Ratings Systems Are Ignored

After the tragic shootings at Columbine High School in 1999, President Clinton asked the Federal Trade Commission (FTC) to investigate whether the motion picture, music, and video game industries advertised and marketed violent material to children and adolescents. Working with industry-provided documents, the FTC determined that, despite the fact that their own ratings systems found the material appropriate only for adults, these industries practiced "pervasive and aggressive marketing of violent movies, music, and electronic games to children."

Many parents find the entertainment industry's media ratings systems difficult to use; 68% of the parents of 10- to 17-year-olds do not use the television rating system at all, and only 10% check the ratings of computer or video games that their adolescents wish to rent or buy. Many parents find the ratings unreliably low, with an objective parental evaluation finding as much as 50% of television shows rated TV-14 to be inappropriate for their teenagers. The ratings are determined by industry-sponsored ratings boards or the artists and producers themselves. They are age based, which assumes that all parents agree with the raters about what is appropriate content for their children of specific ages. Furthermore, different ratings systems for each medium (television, movies, music, and video games) make the ratings confusing, because they have little similarity or relationship to one another. . . .

The strongest single correlate with violent behavior is previous exposure to violence.

Increased Aggression

Research has associated exposure to media violence with a variety of physical and mental health problems for children and adolescents, including aggressive behavior, desensitization to violence, fear, depression, nightmares, and sleep disturbances. More than 3500 research studies have examined the association between media violence and violent behavior; all but 18 have shown a positive relationship. Consistent and strong associations between media exposure and increases in aggression have been found in population-based epidemiologic investigations of violence in American society, cross-cultural studies, experimental and "natural" laboratory research, and longitudinal studies that show that aggressive behavior associated with media exposure persists for decades. The strength of the correlation between media violence and aggressive behavior found on meta-analysis is greater than that of calcium intake and bone mass, lead ingestion and lower IQ, condom nonuse and sexually acquired human immunodeficiency virus infection, or environmental tobacco smoke and lung cancer— associations clinicians accept and on which preventive medicine is based without question.

Children are influenced by media—they learn by observing, imitating, and making behaviors their own. Aggressive attitudes and behaviors are learned by imitating observed models. Research has shown that the strongest single correlate with violent behavior is previous exposure to violence. Because children younger than 8 years cannot discriminate between fantasy and reality, they are uniquely vulnerable to learning and adopting as reality the circumstances, attitudes, and behaviors portrayed by entertainment media.

It is not violence itself but the context in which it is portrayed that can make the difference between learning about violence and learning to be violent. Serious explorations of violence in plays like *Macbeth* and films like *Saving Private Ryan* treat violence as what it is—a human behavior that causes suffering, loss, and sadness to victims and perpetrators. In this context, viewers learn the danger and harm of violence by vicariously experiencing its outcomes. Unfortunately, most entertainment violence is used for immediate visceral thrills without portraying any human cost. Sophisticated special effects, with increasingly graphic depictions of mayhem, make virtual violence more believable and appealing. Studies show that the more realistically violence is portrayed, the greater the likelihood that it will be tolerated and learned. Titillating violence in sexual contexts and comic violence are particularly dangerous, because they associate positive feelings with hurting others.

Studies have shown that after playing video games, young people exhibit measurable decreases in prosocial and helping behaviors.

"Mean World" Syndrome

In addition to modeling violent behavior, entertainment media inflate the prevalence of violence in the world, cultivating in viewers the "mean world" syndrome, a perception of the world as a dangerous place. Fear of being the victim of violence is a strong motivation for some young people to carry a weapon, to be more aggressive, to "get them before they get me." For some children, exposure to media violence leads to anxiety, depression, and posttraumatic stress disorder or to sleep disturbances and nightmares. Some defend media violence as an outlet for vicariously releasing hostility in the safety of virtual reality. However, research testing this "catharsis hypothesis" found that after experiencing media violence, children displayed increased overt aggression because of lowered inhibitions. Numerous studies have shown that the most insidious and potent effect of media violence is to desensitize all of us to real life violence.

Interactive media, such as video games and the Internet, are so new that there has been little time to assess their influence on children's physical and mental health. Early studies of these rapidly growing and ever more sophisticated types of media indicate that the effects of child-initiated virtual violence may be even more profound than those of passive media, such as television. Experimental studies have shown that after playing video games, young people exhibit measurable decreases in prosocial and helping behaviors and increases in aggressive thoughts and violent retaliation to provocation. Playing violent video games has been found to account for a 13% to 22% increase in adolescents' violent behavior; by comparison, smoking tobacco accounts for 14% of the increase in lung cancer.

Children learn by observing and trying out "behavioral scripts." Repeated exposure to violent behavioral scripts can lead to increased feelings of hostility, expectations that others will behave aggressively, desensitization to the pain of others, and increased likelihood of interacting and responding to others with violence. Active participation increases effective learning. Video games are an ideal environment in which to learn violence. They place the player in the role of the aggressor and reward him or her for successful violent behavior. Rather than observing part of a violent interaction, video games allow the player to rehearse an entire behavioral script, from provocation, to choosing to respond violently, to resolution of the conflict. Moreover, video games have been found to be addictive; children and adolescents want to play them for long periods of time to improve their scores and advance to higher levels. Repetition increases their effect.

Interpersonal violence, as victim or as perpetrator, is now a more prevalent health risk than infectious disease, cancer, or congenital disorders for children, adolescents, and young adults. Homicide, suicide, and trauma are leading causes of mortality in the pediatric population, resulting in cumulative death rates of 22.8 per 100,000 in those 5 to 14 years of age and 114.4 per 100,000 in those 15 to 21 years of age. Among urban youth, interpersonal violence is the most prevalent cause of injury (33%), and the incidence of gunshot wounds has increased dramatically [between 1991 and 2001]. Gun violence is now a leading killer of children and adolescents. Each year, 3,500 adolescents are murdered and more than 150,000 adolescents are arrested for violent crimes. Nonwhite children and adolescents, particularly black males, disproportionately suffer the effects of violence in their communities as aggressors and as victims. The number of murderers 15 to 17 years of age increased by 195% between 1984 and 1994, when 94% of juveniles arrested for murder were male and 59% were black. The murder rate of young black males rose 300% during the 3 decades after television's introduction in the United States. Although exposure to media violence is not the sole factor contributing to aggression, antisocial attitudes, and violence among children and adolescents, it is an important health risk factor on which we, as pediatricians and as members of a compassionate society, can intervene.

3

The Problem of Media Violence Is Exaggerated

Andrew O'Hehir

Andrew O'Hehir is a senior writer for Salon.com, an Internet news service. O'Hehir's features and critical writing have appeared in the New York Times, *the* Washington Post, *and the* Village Voice. *He also teaches reporting at New York University.*

Critics have long promoted the belief that media violence breeds violence in society. In recent years, however, that paradigm is losing support. Social scientists and psychologists are drawing attention to the fact that studies of media violence have shown no clear connection to aggression in society. Some experts are examining violent entertainments in past decades and past centuries and demonstrating that people have historically been surrounded by violent and gruesome imagery. Given its omnipresence, then, these researchers are quick to point out the irony that present society is characterized by declining rates of violent crime. Therefore, in this more peaceful era, crusades against media violence are most likely motivated by fears of the media's vast and poorly-understood power, not by fears of a society descending into barbarity.

Kids these days! They're all wasting their spare hours, or so we're told, with immoral trash like "Grand Theft Auto" [GTA], the now-notorious series of slickly decorated and powerfully addictive video games. As Sen. Hillary Clinton explained [in March 2005] at a forum hosted by the Kaiser Family Foundation, "They're playing a game that encourages them to have sex with prostitutes and then murder them."

Fans of "GTA" claim this is a typical non-gamer's misinterpretation—it might be possible to kill hookers in the game, but it won't necessarily help you win—but let's let that go. There's no doubt that "GTA" allows you, for example, to play the role of an ex-con trying to take over a vice-addled city by gunning down drug lords, cops, low-flying aircraft and pretty much everything and everybody else. These games revel in their pseudo-noir amorality, and they're basically designed to be loathed by parents, school principals and tweedy psychologists.

Clinton's attack on the latest manifestation of the Media Demon—you know, the evil force within video games, action movies, rap songs, comic books, dime novels, Judas Priest records played backward and, I don't know, Javanese puppet theater and cave hieroglyphics—is a depressingly familiar ploy in American politics. When you can't make any progress against genuine social problems, or, like Sen. Clinton, you seem religiously committed to triangulating every issue and halving the distance between yourself and [conservative religious leader] Jerry Falwell, you go after the people who sell fantasy to teenagers.

While it's legitimate not to like violent media, ... the case that it directly leads to real-life violence has pretty much collapsed.

Tepid Accusations

What might be most interesting about this latest vapidity, in fact, is what Clinton didn't say. Five years ago, in the wake of the Columbine massacre [school shooting], we were told that there was no serious debate about whether media violence contributed to teenage crime in the real world. A clear link had been established, the case was closed, and the only question was what we were going to do about it. By contrast, Clinton's comments were surprisingly mild and almost entirely subjective. She called violent and debauched entertainment a "silent epidemic," essentially arguing that it has effects, but we don't quite know what they are.

Over the long haul, Clinton said, violent media might teach kids "that it's OK to dis people because they're women or they're a different color or they're from a different place." Perhaps more to the point, she added: "Parents worry their children will not grow up with the same values they did because of the overwhelming presence of the media." That was it—no claims that we were breeding a nation of perverts and murderers, and no mention of all the supposed science indicating a link between simulated mayhem and the real thing. Playing "GTA" and watching Internet porn might lead your kids to "dis" somebody, or to grow up with different values from yours (or anyway to make you concerned that they might). Katy bar the door!

As dopey as Clinton's remarks are, I don't mean to ridicule parents and educators for their legitimate concerns. Of course I'm not certain that violent movies and games (or, for that matter, dumb-ass sitcoms and vapid reality shows) are harmless. My own kids are still too young for this question to matter much, but of course I hold onto the naive hope that they'll spend their formative years hiking the Appalachians and reading about the Byzantine Empire, rather than vegetating in media sludge. But it's long past time to face the fact that while it's legitimate not to like violent media, or to believe it's psychologically deadening in various ways, the case that it directly leads to real-life violence has pretty much collapsed.

Hillary Clinton's equivocation may be something of a compulsive family trait, but it also reflects how muddy this issue has become since the summer of 2000, when the American

Medical Association, the American Psychiatric Association, the American Academy of Child and Adolescent Psychiatry and several other professional busybody organizations issued a joint statement proclaiming that "well over 1,000 studies" had shown a direct connection between media violence and "juvenile aggression." In 2002, Harvard psychologist Steven Pinker wrote that it had become an article of faith "among conservative politicians and liberal health professionals alike . . . that violence in the media is a major cause of American violent crime."

Media-violence research to date has been flawed and inconclusive at best, and a grant-funding scam at worst.

Flawed and Inconclusive Evidence

Actually, there never was any such consensus in the academic fields of psychology, criminology or media studies. And there weren't well over a thousand studies of media violence either—that was one of the many myths and legends that sprung up around this question. In the years since then the mavericks have been increasingly heard from. Even in the theatrical United States Senate hearings convened a few days after the Columbine shootings in 1999, MIT professor Henry Jenkins observed that the idea that violent entertainment had consistent and predictable effects on viewers was "inadequate and simplistic," adding almost poetically that most young people don't absorb entertainment passively, but rather move "nomadically across the media landscape, cobbling together a personal mythology of symbols and stories taken from many different places."

Jenkins was a lonely voice at the time, but more recently the edifice of mainstream certainty has begun to crumble. Psychologists like Pinker, Jonathan Freedman, Jonathan Kellerman and Melanie Moore have counterattacked against their own establishment, arguing that media-violence research to date has been flawed and inconclusive at best, and a grant-funding scam at worst. Some have gone further, suggesting that violent entertainment provides a valuable fantasy outlet for the inevitable rage of childhood and adolescence, and probably helps more children than it hurts. In the teeth of the 1999 hurricane, media scholar Jib Fowles published *The Case for Television Violence*, a dense, dry and devastating dissection that surely counts as one of the most important books about American culture to appear in the last decade. (It's only available from Sage, a small educational publisher, in a paperback edition that costs more than $30—which may tell you something about the mainstream viability of Fowles' message.)

After being eviscerated by Pulitzer-winning journalist Richard Rhodes in his prodigious online article "The Media Violence Myth," even the researcher largely responsible for the exaggerated sense of social consensus on the issue has partially and reluctantly backtracked. In 1986, University of Michigan psychologist L. Rowell Huesmann presented the Senate Judiciary Committee with a dramatic bar graph purporting to show that boys who watched violent TV at age 8 were exceptionally likely to have been convicted of serious crimes by age 30.

The ripple effect of this presentation was tremendous; more than any other single event, it fueled the impression among critics of violent media that they had a scientific case. Huesmann did not admit for many years, until cornered by Rhodes, that the total number of boys he had identified in a Columbia County, N.Y., study who had watched violent TV and then became violent criminals was *three*. A trio of thugs in the boondocks had watched shoot'em-ups as 8-year-olds, and it somehow became a significant statistical finding.

In their lengthy and confusing response to Rhodes' article, Huesmann and his colleague Leonard Eron defend their view that media violence is harmful, arguing that several other studies support theirs. (This is perfectly true. As Fowles' book rigorously demonstrates, the problem with media-violence research as a field is that it reveals no consistent pattern of results, and people on any side of the issue can cherry-pick the studies they like and ignore the others.) In a mixture of brazen overstatement and social-science weasel words, they proclaim that the case "implicating media violence as a risk factor for violent behavior" is as strong as the link between smoking and cancer.

Then comes the bombshell. Near the end of their defense, but before a bizarre personal attack on Rhodes (for being a harsh critic of books he doesn't like, and for taking testosterone supplements), Huesmann and Eron write: "Nowhere have we ever indicated that media violence is the only or even a major cause of violence among youth." I had to read this three times to grasp it: These guys, whose quasi-bogus research subjected us all to a thousand preachy Oprah shows and Joe Lieberman speeches, now say that media violence is *not a major cause* of real-life youth violence. Instead, it's a marginal "risk factor," responsible for no more than 10 percent of the crime rate. (By contrast, Dave Grossman, the retired Marine colonel who is one of the nation's leading anti-media evangelists, claims that media violence is responsible for at least half of all violent crime.)

Examining the Past

We've also heard from criminologists, lawyers and literary scholars as the tide of counterarguments has swelled. The latest of these last is Harold Schechter, a professor at Queens College in New York whose new book, *Savage Pastimes*, provides an eye-opening survey of gruesome entertainment throughout the history of Western civilization. Schechter's main point concerns what scholars call the "periodicity" of campaigns like Sen. Clinton's latest screed. Every time a technological shift occurs (such as from books to movies, radio to TV, movies to video games), he argues, it produces a new medium for gruesome entertainment aimed at adolescent audiences, and produces a renewed outrage among the self-appointed guardians of civilization. . . .

The Jeremiahs who condemn violent entertainment, whether crime comics or "Grand Theft Auto," also invariably lament the passage of a golden age, generally contemporaneous with their own childhoods, when entertainment was healthful and wholesome, suitable for infants and grannies alike. I don't mean to impugn Granny, who may have a healthy appetite for phony bloodshed, but these moral guardians' sunny views of the past either reflect fuzzy memories or whopping hypocrisy.

Schechter offers an amusing catalog of the outrageous bloodshed and mayhem found in popular entertainment since time immemorial, from the classics (as he observes, the on-stage blinding of Gloucester in "King Lear"—"out, vile jelly"—is one of the most traumatic acts of violence in any medium) to the pornographic sadism of Grand-Guignol theater, the lurid sensationalism of turn-of-the-century "penny papers" and the ugly misogyny of Mickey Spillane's best-selling pulp novels. Undoubtedly Hillary Clinton would prefer that today's kids read books instead of playing "GTA," and Schechter might suggest *Seth Jones: or, The Captives of the Frontier*, a wilderness adventure that was one of the best-selling kids' books of the 19th century. In one scene, the hero comes upon the corpse of a man who has been tied to a tree by Indians and burned to death:

"Every vestige of the flesh was burned off to the knees, and the bones, white and glistening, dangled to the crisp and blackened members above! The hands, tied behind, had passed through the fire unscathed, but every other part of the body was literally roasted!" Seth is greatly relieved, however, to discover that the victim was not a white man. As Schechter says, it's impossible to imagine anyone publishing this as kiddie lit today, both for its gore quotient and its casual racism. . . .

Schechter knows what you're thinking: At least those kids were reading, and as reprehensible by our standards as those books may have been, there's really no comparison between the printed page and the "hyperkinetic visuals of movies and computer games." The only answer to this is maybe and maybe not; critics of pop culture always assume that new technologies have rendered kids incapable of telling the difference between reality and fantasy, and so far they've always been wrong. Schechter writes that for children who had never seen a movie or a video game, "the printed page *was* a PlayStation, and penny dreadfuls were state-of-the-art escapism, capable of eliciting a shudder or thrill every bit as intense as the kind induced by today's high-tech entertainment." The relativist position that each generation is equally affected by the media available to it is supported by ample historical evidence, from the way that the audiences at early film screenings rose in panic when on-screen trains bore down upon them to the wildly Dionysian effect of that hypersexual, morals-corroding music, swing.

If Sen. Clinton might prefer an outdoor family activity in the sunny American heartland, there's always the example of Owensboro, Ky., where on Aug. 14, 1936, some 20,000 citizens of all ages crowded into the courthouse square. It was a "jolly holiday," according to newspaper reports. Hot dogs, popcorn and soft drinks were sold, and there was a mixture of cheers and catcalls—but no general disorder, as the local paper angrily insisted—when sheriff's deputies brought a man named Rainey Bethea out to the scaffold, where he was hanged.

The Bethea execution, with its clear subtext of white supremacy (Bethea was a black man convicted of raping a white woman, and the crowd of onlookers was entirely white, except for the undertakers commissioned to retrieve his body), caused a national scandal, and pretty much brought an end to one of the Western world's most enduring entertainment traditions. In medieval and early modern Europe, public executions were major carnival attractions, and high-profile criminals were dispatched with loving sadism and a truly diabolical degree of invention. . . .

Times Have Changed

Schechter doesn't bring up the Bethea execution to paint white Kentuckians of the Depression as depraved rubes; his point is that we actually have come a long way in seven decades. We're free to regard violent movies and video games as loathsome, but we also have to admit they reflect at least a partially successful sublimation of what William James called "our aboriginal capacity for murderous excitement." Few of us are eager for the return of public executions (except perhaps the programming executives at Fox) and no real cops or prostitutes were harmed during the creation of "Grand Theft Auto." Although a few juveniles charged with murder, or their victims' families, have argued that video games were responsible for murder, kids who play video-game shooters aren't outside gunning down the neighbors, possibly because that would mean getting off their butts and leaving behind the overlit universe of their TV or computer screen.

Our pop culture is less bloody-minded than that of the past.

Was Past Entertainment Less Violent?

As Schechter says, there are two linked assumptions that underpin all the hysteria about purported media-influenced violence in the last 20 years, if not longer. Assumption No. 1 is that we live in an especially violent time in human history, surrounded by serial killers, hardened teenage "superpredators," genocidal atrocities and all sorts of amoral mayhem. Assumption No. 2 is that our popular entertainment is far more violent than the entertainment of the past, and presents that violence in more graphic and bloodthirsty detail. For critics of media violence, from the Clintons to Dave Grossman to the leadership of the child-psychiatry establishment, these assumptions go essentially unchallenged, and the conclusion they draw is that there is a causal or perhaps circular relationship between these "facts": Media violence breeds real violence, which leads to ever more imaginative media violence, and so on.

A longtime crime buff who has written several books about notorious murderers, Schechter mounts an impressive case in *Savage Pastimes* that, if anything, our pop culture is less bloody-minded than that of the past. Anyone who looks back at the 1950s, when Schechter himself was a child, and remembers only *Leave It to Beaver* and Pat Boone needs to read his discourse on the hugely popular *Davy Crockett* miniseries of 1954, "whose level of carnage," he writes, "remains unsurpassed in the history of televised children's entertainment." This series, with its barrage of "shootings, stabbings, scalpings, stranglings," was broadcast on Wednesday nights at 7:30 p.m., and presented as the acme of wholesome family fare.

Violence has clearly been decreasing in the Western world for the last 500 years.

In fact, as Schechter demonstrates, '50s TV was profoundly rooted in guns and gunfire, to a degree that would provoke widespread outrage today. But there are factors he doesn't consider, or considers only in passing, that fuel people's perceptions that the past was less violent, both in real and symbolic terms. Those '50s TV shows were mostly westerns, of course, which meant that they presented themselves as instructive fables of American history in its most masculine, individualistic form. They were racially and politically uncomplicated; *Gunsmoke* and *Bonanza* developed a social conscience in the '60s, but the white screen cowboys of the '50s were heroes, and the whites, Indians and Mexicans around them were clearly divided into good guys and bad.

In other words, while *Davy Crockett* and *Have Gun Will Travel* and *The Rifleman* were loaded with violence, it was mostly reassuring violence, presented without splatter and without moral consequences. The graphic media violence of our age, whether in *Taxi Driver* or *Reservoir Dogs* or *CSI* or "Grand Theft Auto," is deliberately unsettling, meant to fill viewers with dread and remind them that life is an uncertain, morally murky affair. This might put us closer to the murder-obsessed Victorian age than to the scrubbed '50s, and in examining both eras it's important to remember that this message can be delivered badly or well, used for a cheap roller-coaster effect or a tremendous "King Lear" catharsis. (It's also worth pointing out that Jib Fowles disagrees with Schecter, arguing, "It does appear that television violence has been slowly growing in volume and intensity since 1950.")

A More Peaceful Era

But if Assumption No. 2 looks questionable, Assumption No. 1 is just flat-out false. As Fowles painstakingly details in *The Case for Television Violence*, violence has clearly been decreasing in the Western world for the last 500 years; as far as we can tell from uneven record-keeping, the murder rate in medieval Europe was several times higher than it is today, even in relatively violent societies like the U.S. While the 20th century has seen some spikes in violent crime—correlating less to the arrival of television than to the proportion of young men in the population—the downward trend since about 1980 has reinforced the general tendency. As Rhodes puts it, "We live in one of the least violent eras in peacetime human history."

Again, there are some complicating ambiguities here, although they don't make the absolute numbers look any different. If you're convinced that we live amid a psychotic crime wave, well, blame the media. Murder has become an increasingly rare crime, and most of it is pretty unglamorous—poor people, many of them black and brown, killing each other in petty disputes over love affairs or insultingly small amounts of money. But whenever something truly ghoulish happens—a serial killer hacks up some white girls or a mom drowns her kids in the tub—we're exposed to so many pseudo-news stories and movies of the week that it seems as if society is totally out of its gourd and such things are happening every day.

I don't think there's any question that the sense of dislocation this produces, while unmeasurable by social science, can be profound. We know this as the "mean world" syndrome, and it's the reason why, for instance, my wife's 90-something grandparents not only don't go outside after dark, but also refuse to answer the phone. (Apparently the depraved criminals roaming the suburban streets can teleport themselves through the phone lines.) Our obsession with violent crime may indeed be at an all-time high, even as crime itself keeps becoming rarer. Perhaps TV has made us so frightened that we've mostly stopped killing each other.

We know that the media . . . is tremendously powerful, but we don't understand its power, so we fear it.

There's far more that one could and perhaps should say about the essentially adolescent character of our civilization, fatally torn between the impulses of Eros and Thanatos. But the point I'm struggling toward is that while you can't prove that media violence *doesn't* lead to real violence—and only an idiot would assert that no one has ever been inspired to commit a crime by a book or movie or video game—our definitions of "media" and "violence" may need some rethinking. And as a general proposition, the simplistic consensus of a few years ago stands on exceedingly shaky ground. "This whole episode of studying television violence," as Fowles told Rhodes in 2000, "is going to be seen by history as a travesty. It's going to be used in classes as an example of how social science can just go totally awry." ...

Scaring People Straight

Attorney and author Marjorie Heins has pointed out that the conflict between pop culture and its critics is literally as old as Western civilization: Plato thought that unsavory art should be censored, while Aristotle argued that violent and upsetting drama had a cathartic effect, and helped purge the undesirable emotions of spectators. Jib Fowles suggests that these periodic culture wars are mostly a way of displacing anxieties about class, race and gender, as well as, most obviously, a proxy war between middle-aged adults and the succeeding generations whose culture they can't quite understand.

Perhaps the most sensible words on this subject that I've discovered come from comics author Gerard Jones, in a 2000 *Mother Jones* article that became, in part, the basis for his book *Killing Monsters*. "I'm not going to argue that violent entertainment is harmless," he wrote. "I am going to argue that it's helped hundreds of people for every one it's hurt, and that it can help far more if we learn to use it well. I am going to argue that our fear of 'youth violence' isn't well-founded on reality, and that the fear can do more harm than the reality. We act as though our highest priority is to prevent our children from growing up into murderous thugs—but modern kids are far more likely to grow up too passive, too distrustful of themselves, too easily manipulated."

That expresses, I suspect, exactly what many parents of more or less my generation feel about their kids and the media. To be fair, I also think it's a more honest, less red-state-coded version of what Hillary Clinton was trying to say. We know that the media stew most of us marinate in is tremendously powerful, but we don't understand its power, so we fear it. Furthermore, even if violent entertainment has always been with us, as Harold Schechter argues, it's *supposed* to scare us, because it calls up emotions and impulses we don't usually want to think about, because it summons demons from below our conscious minds and before our approved history. That's its job.

Ultimately, we can't protect our kids from being frightened or unsettled by things they will inevitably encounter, whether while reading Dostoevsky or playing the latest zombie-splattering incarnation of *Resident Evil*. We can't stop them from forging their own culture out of fragments and shards they collect along the way, a culture specifically intended to confuse and alienate us. But I think Jones is right: Most of us don't have to worry about breeding little homicidal maniacs. What's far more plausible, and more dangerous, is that we'll raise a pack of sedentary, cynical little button-pushing consumption monsters who never go outside. Now that's scary.

4

Television Violence Is a Serious Problem for Children

Parents Television Council

Founded in 1995, the Parents Television Council (PTC) is a national grassroots organization to combat the influence of television violence on children. The PTC advises parents on shaping the television viewing habits of their children. The organization also lobbies legislators and industry leaders for decency standards in broadcasting.

The impact of television violence upon young people is well documented. The average child watches 25 hours of television per week, and much of the programming has violent content. Indeed, most television broadcasters have done little to stem the flow of televised violence or even limit its appearance to late evening programming. Instead, violence is routinely displayed during family viewing times. This overload of violence leads many young people to believe that society itself is violent and that violence is a way to resolve life's difficulties. Unfortunately, society and young people will continue to suffer from the negative effects of such learned behavior if broadcasters or federal lawmakers do not make an effort to reduce the amount of violence on television.

Concerns about the impact of television violence on society are almost as old as the medium itself. As early as 1952, the United States House of Representatives was holding hearings to explore the impact of television violence and concluded that the "television broadcast industry was a perpetrator and a deliverer of violence." In 1972 the Surgeon General's office conducted an overview of existing studies on television violence and concluded that it was "a contributing factor to increases in violent crime and antisocial behavior." In his testimony to the U.S. Senate Subcommittee on Communications, Surgeon General Jesse Steinfeld said, "It is clear to me that the causal relationship between televised violence and antisocial behavior is sufficient to warrant appropriate and immediate remedial action . . . There comes a time when the data are sufficient to justify action. That time has come."

Over the years, there have been literally hundreds of studies examining the connection between media violence and violence in real-life, the results of which were summarized in a joint statement signed by representatives from six of the nation's top public health organizations, including the American Academy of Pediatrics, the American Psychological Association, and the American Medical Association: "Well over 1000 studies . . . point overwhelmingly to a causal connection between media violence and aggressive behavior in some children. The conclusion of the public health community, based on over 30 years of research, is that viewing entertainment violence can lead to increases in aggressive attitudes, values and behavior, particularly in children."

Television reaches children at a younger age and for more time than any other socializing influence, except family.

Today, the connection between media violence and aggressive and violent behavior in real life has been so well documented, that for many, the question is settled. In fact, a position paper by the American Psychiatric Association on media violence begins by declaring: "The debate is over." According to Jeffrey McIntyre, legislative and federal affairs officer for the American Psychological Association, "To argue against it is like arguing against gravity." . . .

The Impact of Media Violence

Television can be profoundly influential in shaping an impressionable child or adolescent's values, attitudes, perceptions, and behaviors. Television reaches children at a younger age and for more time than any other socializing influence, except family. The average child spends 25 hours a week watching television, more time than they spend in school or engaged in any other activity except sleep. Is it any wonder then that children so readily absorb the messages that are presented to them?

So what is the cumulative impact of 25 hours of television a week?

It is estimated that by the time an average child leaves elementary school, he or she will have witnessed 8,000 murders and over 100,000 other acts of violence. By the time that child is 18 years-of-age, he or she will witness 200,000 acts of violence, including 40,000 murders. One 17-year longitudinal study concluded that teens who watched more than one hour of TV a day were almost four times as likely as other teens to commit aggressive acts in adulthood.

Witnessing repeated violent acts increases general feelings of hostility.

Television teaches viewers—especially young viewers, who have more difficulty discriminating between real life and fantasy—that violence is the accepted way we solve problems. Moreover, studies show that the more real-life the violence portrayed, the greater the likelihood that it will be learned.

And while it's true that not every child who is exposed to a lot of televised violence is going to grow up to be violent, "every exposure to violence increases the chances that some day a child will behave more violently than they otherwise would," according to Dr. L. Rowell Huesmann of the University of Michigan.

Violent entertainment leaves a mark, even on children who don't engage in aggressive behaviors. Witnessing repeated violent acts increases general feelings of hostility and can lead to desensitization and a lack of empathy for human suffering. Over time, consumption of violence-laden imagery can leave viewers with the perception that they are living in a mean and dangerous world, giving them an unrealistically dark view of life.

For children who *do* act out aggressively, the results can be deadly. Week after week, newspapers are filled with blood-chilling accounts of children committing copy-cat crimes inspired by the latest horror film or violent video game.

In the past couple of years, attention to this issue [of television violence] all but disappeared.

The Slippery Slope of TV Violence

Entertainment violence is a slippery slope. With repeated exposure, even the most gruesome and grisly depictions of violence eventually seem tame. In time, viewers become desensitized, so Hollywood has to keep pushing the envelope in order to elicit the same reaction.

Lt. Col. David Grossman, author of *Stop Teaching Our Kids to Kill*, explains: "Violence is like the nicotine in cigarettes. The reason why the media has to pump ever more violence into us is because we've built up a tolerance. In order to get the same high, we need ever-higher levels . . . the television industry has gained its market share through an addictive and toxic ingredient."

Yet, despite the mountains of research, the consensus of the medical community, and a growing list of casualties from copy-cat crimes, Hollywood continues to produce increasingly graphic and gory entertainment products, all the while denying any culpability for the violent behaviors their products inspire.

Popular entertainment came under intense scrutiny after the tragic April 1999 massacre at Columbine High School, as published reports pointing to the Columbine killers' fondness for first-person-shooter video games and the eerie similarities between the murders and certain violent films began to emerge. There were a handful of media mea culpas as some in the entertainment industry grudgingly conceded that there might be a loose connection to violent entertainment products. Even CBS President Leslie Moonves conceded "anyone who thinks the media has nothing to do with [the bloodshed at Columbine] is an idiot."

But has anything really changed? Is television today [in 2003] any less violent than it was in 1999? In the past couple of years, attention to this issue all but disappeared as our national consciousness has, understandably, turned to external threats. Has Hollywood taken advantage of this paradigm shift to start reintroducing violent content to prime time network television?

The PTC Study

PTC analysts examined all prime time entertainment series on the major broadcast television networks (ABC, CBS, Fox, NBC, UPN and the WB) from the first two weeks of the 1998, 2000, and 2002 November sweeps periods. The ITV network was not included in this analysis because the network was launched just a few months before the first study period and had limited original programming in 1998 and 2000. A total of 400 program hours were analyzed.

Television broadcasts of movies, news, and sports programs were not included in this analysis.

In qualitative terms, television violence seemed to have become more graphic over time [from 1998–2002].

PTC analysts reviewed the programs for all instances of violence. Mild forms of violence included threats of violence, mayhem or pyrotechnics (fires, explosions, car crashes), deaths implied, and fist fights or martial arts fights. More extreme examples of violence included use of guns or other weapons, depiction of blood, graphic depictions (e.g. a dismembered body), deaths depicted, and torture.

- Overall, violence increased in every time slot between 1998 and 2002. On all the networks combined, violence was 41% more frequent during the 8:00 p.m. (ET/PT) Family Hour in 2002 than in 1998.

- UPN and Fox had the highest rate of violence during the Family Hour in 2002, with 7.5 and 4.67 instances per hour respectively. ABC had the largest percentage increase during the Family Hour, going from .13 instances per hour in 1998 to 2 instances per hour in 2002 (an increase of more than 1400%).

- The WB and CBS had the least violence, both in terms of absolute numbers and per-hour rates during the Family Hour in 2002, with .11 and .21 instances per hour respectively.

- CBS and the WB were also the only networks to show any improvement during the Family Hour. CBS reduced Family Hour violence by 73.4%, going from a rate of .79 instances of violence per hour in 1998 to .21 instances per hour in 2002. The WB network went from 2.5 instances of violence per hour during the

Family Hour in 1998 to 2.08 instances per hour in 2000, to .11 instances per hour in 2002. Overall, WB showed a 95.6% decrease in violence from 1998 to 2002. That drop can be attributed almost entirely to the fact that *Buffy the Vampire Slayer* moved from the WB network to UPN in 2001.

- During the second hour of prime time (9–10:00 p.m. ET/PT), violence was 134.4% more frequent in 2002 than in 1998. During the third hour of prime time (10–11:00 p.m. ET/PT) violent content was nearly 63% more common in 2002 than in 1999.

- Violent content was found to become more common in later hours of prime time. Violence was 149% more frequent during the second hour of prime time than during the Family Hour in 2002. Fights were 16% more common; graphic depictions increased in frequency from .02 instances per hour during the Family Hour to .54 instances per hour during the 9:00 p.m. (ET/PT) time slot; and depictions of death increased from .13 instances per hour to .87 during the second hour of prime time.

- The WB, UPN, and CBS had the highest per-hour rates for violence during the second hour of prime time. On the WB, violence spiked from an average of 1 instance per hour in 1998 to 6.7 instances per hour in 2002 (an increase of 570%). UPN had the largest increase, going from .13 instances per hour in 1998 to 6.6 instances per hour in 2002 (an increase of nearly 5,000%). CBS had the smallest increase, with 5 instances per hour in 1998 and 6.5 instances of violence per hour in 2002 for an increase of 30%. NBC was the only network to improve during the second hour of prime time, going from 3.14 instances of violence per hour in 1998 to 1.33 instances per hour in 2002 for a decrease of 57.6%.

- Only three broadcast networks continue their program feed into the 10:00 hour: ABC, CBS, and NBC. All three of those networks showed a small increase in depictions of violence during that hour from 1998 to 2002. ABC aired 27% more violence in 2002; CBS aired 37.8% more violence; and NBC aired 78.5% more violence in 2002 than in 1998. CBS had the highest rate of violence during the 10:00 hour in 2002 at 8.1 instances per hour. ABC had the lowest, at 3 instances per hour.

- In qualitative terms, television violence seemed to have become more graphic over time. In 1998 the most common form of TV violence during all hours of prime time was fist fights or martial arts fights (where no one was killed). By 2002, these relatively mild fight sequences became less frequent and were supplanted by more frequent use of guns or other weapons. In 1998, 44% of all violent scenes during the Family Hour were mild fight sequences compared to 32% in 2002. In 1998, 29% of all violent sequences included the use of guns or other weapons. By 2002, that number increased to 38%.

Related Findings

- Use or depictions of blood in violent scenes were more common in the Family Hour in 2002 than in 2000 on ABC, NBC, and UPN (there were no depictions of blood within the study period in 1998 during the Family Hour). Fox had no change (with .33 instances per hour both years), and CBS and WB actually presented fewer violent scenes with blood in 2002 than in 2000.

- Looking at the second hour of prime time, violent scenes containing depictions of blood were 141% more common in 2002 than in 1998. ABC, CBS, Fox, and UPN all had more frequent depictions of blood during this time slot in 2002 than in 1998. NBC had 31.2% fewer depictions of blood in 2002 than in 1998.

• On the whole, the use of guns and other weapons in Family Hour programs increased by 85.1% between 1998 and 2002, although some individual networks did show some improvement. ABC, Fox, and UPN all had more scenes containing guns or other weapons in 2002 than in 1998, NBC, CBS, and the WB had fewer.

• During the second hour of prime time there was a 200% increase in scenes depicting the use of guns or other weapons between 1998 and 2002. NBC was the only network to reduce the frequency of such scenes during this time slot by 2002. CBS remained constant at 1.4 instances per hour of gun play or use of other weapons in both 1998 and 2002.

• The per-hour rate of deaths depicted has slowly climbed since 1998 in every time slot. During the Family Hour in 1998, there were .06 deaths depicted per hour. By 2002, that number reached .13. During the second hour of prime time in 1998, there were .35 deaths depicted per hour. By 2002, it had increased to .87. During the 10:00 p.m. (ET/PT) time slot, deaths depicted per hour rose from .23 to 1.7.

Examples of Televised Violence—1998

Examples from 8–9:00 p.m. ET/PT Time Slot

Brimstone—11/06/98 8:00 p.m. Fox. A rapist who escaped from hell comes into a woman's bedroom wearing a devil mask. He wrestles with the woman, tossing her into a glass table, then onto the bed. He jumps on top of her on the bed. She is holding a gun, and shoots him several times in the chest at point blank range. The gun shots have no effect on him. It is implied that he goes on to rape her. [Later in the show] Zeke attempts to send the rapist back to hell by shooting him in the eyes, but to no avail. Zeke later corners the rapist. He picks up a garden spade and is shown thrusting it downward several times (presumably into the rapist's head, thereby destroying his eyes and sending him back to hell).

Buffy the Vampire Slayer—11/17/98 8:00 p.m. WB. Buffy beheads a demon with a battle axe.

Examples from 9–10:00 p.m. ET/PT Time Slot

The X-Files—11/15/98 9:00 p.m. Fox. A woman bangs her head against the glass window of a police car. All of a sudden, blood spatters against the window and the woman collapses in the back seat of the police car. Investigators discover that her head exploded.

Millennium—11/06/98 9:00 p.m. Fox. Agent Hollis walks into an empty house. In a back room she finds what appears to be an autopsy table. She goes through another door, and finds a room that appears to be covered in blood. There is a hose of some kind that is dripping blood, the walls appear to be coated in blood, and on the wall there is a meat hook. On a table she sees a pair of bloody gloves, bloody knives, etc. . . . There is a tub that appears to be full of blood. Hollis sees a skull on a table. . . .

Examples of Televised Violence—2000

Examples from 8–9:00 p.m. ET/PT Time Slot

Buffy the Vampire Slayer—11/14/00 8:00 p.m. WB. Buffy fights a vampire in the graveyard. She kicks him to the ground. She then knocks him onto a gravestone. When Buffy goes to stake him, he pushes the stake into her abdomen. Buffy is shown again with the stake in her. There is blood on her sweater and her hands. We see her pull the stake out of her body.

Boston Public—11/13/00 8:00 p.m. Fox. Two boys get in a fight in the classroom. One of the boys bites a piece of the other boy's ear off. The victim stands up, blood running all over his shirt. The biter spits the piece of ear out of his mouth and it hits Harvey in the forehead.

Examples from 9–10:00 p.m. ET/PT Time Slot

City of Angels—11/02/00 9:00 p.m. CBS. Damon goes into Gwen's house and attacks her. She is only wearing a bra and panties and she screams for help. He throws her against the bed and gets on top of her. He smacks her across the face. He chokes her and continues to beat her on the face. Gwen's brother Curtis comes into the house and attacks Damon. They beat on each other and glass breaks and they use lamps and pieces of furniture to hit each other. Damon pulls a knife on Curtis. Curtis flips Damon off the balcony and Damon falls below, dead. Damon is shown dead on the ground and there's a large pool of blood under his face.

C.S.I.—11/10/00 9:00 p.m. CBS. There is a flashback of Amy killing Fay. Fay is thrown into a big fish tank. After Fay falls to the floor, Amy hits her in the head with a pick axe. . . .

Examples of Televised Violence—2002
Examples from 8–9:00 p.m. ET/PT Time Slot

Buffy the Vampire Slayer—11/05/02 8:00 p.m. WB. Buffy and a demon are fighting. She throws a hatchet at him, which becomes planted in his chest. He falls to the ground.

Providence—11/01/02 8:00 p.m. NBC. A man is shown with a knife in his chest. Blood is spreading around the wound. Kim yanks the knife out of the man's chest.

Charmed—11/10/02 8:00 p.m. WB. A warlock named Bacarra needs a fresh human heart to complete his potion to vanquish the witches. He puts a witch to sleep and takes her heart out while she is still alive. Her eyes widen as Bacarra reaches into her chest. The sounds of his hand penetrating her flesh can be heard. He is shown holding her heart in his hand.

Examples from 9–10:00 p.m. ET/PT Time Slot

C.S.I.—10/31/02 9:00 p.m. CBS. Gil cuts a finger off of a man's dead body, takes out the bone, puts the finger over one of his own and makes a fingerprint with it.

The District—11/02/02 9:00 p.m. CBS. In a flashback sequence a man inside a subway kills Mannion's friend by shooting him at point-blank range. . . .

It is sadly apparent that broadcasters no longer have any interest in showing respect for the American home.

Failure to Send Good Messages

Television is an invited guest into the family home, and for that reason, broadcasters have a special obligation to take care with the messages and images they present. There was a time when broadcasters took that obligation seriously. Until fairly recently, television broadcasters adhered to a voluntary code of conduct, the Television Code, which was rooted in a desire to show the "highest standards of respect for the American home."

Even though the code fell out of use more than twenty years ago, it is sadly apparent that broadcasters no longer have any interest in showing respect for the American home. They have used the broadcast airwaves to deliver messages that poison impressionable young minds. Despite the obvious concerns of millions of parents, public policy and medical experts, depictions of violence on prime time broadcast television have become more common and increasingly graphic, and there doesn't appear to be an end in sight. Broadcasters will continue to push the envelope with TV violence as long and as far as they are able. The only way to reverse this trend is for viewers to push back. . . .

Lawmakers have been concerned with the problem of media violence since 1952, but there are no laws on the books prohibiting or restricting depictions of violence on television. Without an enforcement mechanism, Congress has no real power to force the entertainment industry to address the problem. Perhaps it is time, as Senator Sam Brownback and FCC [Federal Communications Commission] commissioner Michael Copps suggested [in 2003], for the FCC to make a priority of reducing TV violence and to expand the definition of broadcast indecency to include violence.

5

Television Is Unfairly Blamed for Violence in Society

Jonathan L. Freedman

Jonathan L. Freedman is a professor of psychology at the University of Toronto. He is the author of Social Psychology *and* Media Violence and Its Effect on Aggression.

Television has become a prime scapegoat for violence in society. Most people are certain that violence on television inspires people—most commonly children—to imitate what they see and bring about chaos, tragedy, or even death. However, in some of the most heinous cases of youth violence, television has been cleared of any negative influence. Regardless of the evidence, society is still convinced that the world has become a dangerous place and that television is a significant cause of this climate of aggression and fear. This unfortunate belief persists even though rates of violent crime have been declining for decades and youth crime has also reached a statistical low point. Television should not be so easily blamed for violence in society when other social maladies may lie at the root of the problem.

On 14 October 1992 the headlines in many American papers read BOY LIGHTS FIRE THAT KILLS SISTER. Two days earlier a television program had shown young boys setting fires. The very next day, Tommy Jones (not his real name) an eight-year-old boy, set a fire that burned down the trailer in which he and his family lived. His baby sister was trapped inside and burned to death. All over the United States, newspapers, television stations, and politicians concluded that Tommy must have seen the television program and gotten the idea of playing with matches and setting a fire. Surely this was a perfect example of why children should not be allowed to watch violent programs.

In February 1993 the whole world shuddered at an awful crime committed by two young boys in England. That month a small boy who was about to turn three was taken from a shopping mall in Liverpool by two ten-year-old boys. Jamie Bulger had walked away from his mother for only a second— long enough for Jon Venables to take his hand and lead him out of the mall with his friend Robert Thompson. They took Jamie on a walk of over two-and-a-half miles, along the way stopping every now and again to torture the poor little boy, who was crying constantly for his mommy. Finally they left his beaten small body on the tracks so that a train could run him over.

Jamie's frantic mother noticed almost at once that he was missing, and a massive search began. Jon and Robert were identified from surveillance tapes in the mall. At first they denied any knowledge of Jamie, but eventually they admitted everything and led police to the dead body. Although they confessed to taking Jamie, each accused the other of doing the torturing and killing. During the trial, Jon cried a lot and looked miserable, while Robert seemed unaffected. They were convicted and sentenced to long prison terms.

The trial judge had observed the boys for many days and heard all the testimony. At the sentencing he denounced them as inhuman monsters. He also said he was convinced that one of the causes of their crime was television violence. According to the judge, shortly before the crime the boys had watched a television program, involving kidnapping and murder. They had imitated this program and the result was Jamie's kidnapping, torture, and murder. It was, he said, one more case of the harmful effects of television violence.

The ordinary occurrences of fighting in imitation of television heroes have convinced many people that television causes aggression.

Seeing Is Believing

People think they see the effects of media violence in their daily lives: Every day, parents and teachers watch children practising martial arts at home and in schoolyards. Pass by a playground and you will see martial arts in action—slashing arms, jumps, kicks, the works. A generation ago young boys almost never used karate kicks; now they all do. And this goes along with increased violence in our schools. Again, surely television violence has caused it.

The terrible crimes related to television programs, the increase in violent crime since the introduction of television, and the ordinary occurrences of fighting in imitation of television heroes have convinced many people that television violence causes aggression, violence and crime. It seems so obvious that there is no need to worry about the scientific evidence. Why should anyone care what the research shows?

Don't be so sure. Not so terribly long ago it was obvious that the world was flat, that the sun revolved around the earth, and that the longer women stayed in bed after childbirth the healthier they would be. Scientific research has proven all of these wrong. An awful lot of people also knew that men were smarter than women, that picking babies up when they cried would only encourage them to cry more in the future, and that rewarding kids for playing games would make them like the games more. Research has proven all of these wrong too. Perhaps it will do the same for beliefs about the effects of media violence—that is why so many people have done so much research to establish whether watching violent programs really does make children more aggressive.

Deflating False Claims

Anecdotes are not always very reliable. Let's look at the examples I offered above. Consider the case of the fire that killed the little girl. At first glance there seems no question what happened. The newspapers all reported that the boy was a well-behaved child who had never been in trouble before. He happened to watch the TV program about setting fires, and he imitated what he saw. What more could one ask? Clearly, this was a simple case of TV causing a tragedy.

But it wasn't. As those reporters who looked into the incident more carefully found out, the truth was quite different from the early reports. First of all, little Tommy was not a very well-behaved boy. He had been playing with matches and setting fires for some time—long before the program was aired. No one had been killed or hurt in any of the fires before this, so they did not make the news, but they were set nonetheless. Second, and more important, the TV program in question was shown only on cable, not on the regular networks. *And Tommy's family did not have cable television.* In fact, no one in the trailer park had it, and no one he knew had it. *So there was no way he could have seen the show.* The tragic incident had nothing whatsoever to do with the television program that had been shown the day before. Rather than it being a case of television causing the tragedy, it was simply one more instance of children playing with fire and someone getting hurt.

Also consider the case of the two boys who killed Jamie Bulger. The judge announced in court that he was convinced that TV played a crucial role in the crime—that the boys had watched a program about kidnapping and had imitated it. Again, an obvious case of TV violence producing violence?

Yet the judge's belief had no basis in fact. The police made it absolutely clear that the boys had not watched the program in question, that they did not watch television much, and that there was no reason to believe that TV had anything to do with the crime. The last time children of this age had been found guilty of murder in England had been several hundred years earlier. It hadn't been due to television then, so why in the world would the judge think so this time? This was a horrific crime beyond human comprehension. We have no idea how they could have committed it, but there is not the slightest bit of evidence that it was caused by television.

The availability of television in the United States and Canada coincided with vast changes in our societies.

Social Changes Accompanied the Advent of Television

Yes, the rate of violent crime increased after television was introduced. But there is no reason to think the two are in any way related. . . . Television was also introduced to France, Germany, Italy, and Japan at around the same time as it came to the United States and Canada. Yet crime rates did not increase in these other countries. If television violence were causing the increase, surely it should have had the same effect elsewhere. We have to remember that the availability of television in the United States and Canada coincided with vast changes in our societies. Between 1960 and 1985—the period of the increase in crime—the divorce rate more than doubled, many more single parents and women began working outside the home, the use of illegal drugs increased, the gap between rich and poor grew, and because of the postwar baby boom, there was a sharp increase in the number of young males. Almost all of the experts, including police, criminologists, and sociologists, agree that these factors played a crucial role in the increase in crime, and no one seriously blames television for these changes in society. It is an accident, a coincidence, that television ownership increased during this same period. These important social changes are certainly some of the causes of the increase in crime; television ownership may be irrelevant.

Although it may seem as if youth violence is increasing, it is actually declining. In 1999 the rate of murder by white youths in California was at a record low, 65 per cent less than in 1970, and the rates for Black, Latino, and Asian youths were also low. According to FBI records, elementary-school students are much less likely to murder today than they were in the 1960s and 1970s. And, both Black and white children feel less menaced now by violence in their schools than twenty-five years ago. True, over the past seven years there has been an increase in incidents in schools in which more than one person was killed. However, the number of children killed in schools in the United States and Canada has dropped during the same period, from a high of fifty-five in the 1992–93 school year to sixteen in 1998–99. This last year included one killing in Canada, which shocked a country not used to this kind of violence in its schools, but it is the only case of its kind in this decade.

Moreover, the rates for all violent crimes have been dropping steadily and dramatically since the early 1990s. The number of homicides in the big American cities has plunged to levels not seen since the early 70s, and the numbers for other violent crimes have been falling as well. This, at a time when movies and television shows are as violent as ever. Add to this the rising popularity of rap music, with its violent language and themes; and of video games, which are just as violent and just as popular. If violence in the media causes aggression, how can real-life evidence and crime be dropping?

None of this proves that television violence plays no role in aggression and violence. The point is that stories about its effects are often false and that obvious effects may be explainable in other ways.

6

Film and Television Violence Is Likely to Get More Graphic

David Hiltbrand

David Hiltbrand is a staff writer for the Philadelphia Inquirer. *He writes feature columns as well as music and television reviews.*

Media violence is becoming more graphic, and film and television are in the vanguard of this trend. Beheadings and other vicious murders are portrayed in slow motion in many grisly movies, and torture is commonplace in many prime time television programs. The rise in explicitness is due to competition between movies and shows for more such sensational content. It is also a result of desensitized audiences that have been raised on violent media content and are no longer shocked by tamer displays. Entertainment industries are self-regulated and seem unwilling to censor screen violence, especially because the more gruesome movies and television programs enjoy brisk aftermarket DVD sales. Therefore, with audience appeal and healthy incomes, screen violence will likely continue to push beyond all restraints.

Greetings from the slaughterhouse that is pop culture.

Our most popular forms of entertainment—TV, films and books—have followed video games into a ferocious new realm of ultraviolence marked by increasingly graphic depictions of brutality.

Consider:

- In an episode of the Fox network's *Killer Instinct*, a home-surgery victim wakes up on his patio to find his liver cooking on the gas grill.

- In *Domino*, in theaters [in 2005], bounty hunters shoot off a man's arm and then carry the severed limb around with them.

- In [2004's] sadistic film *Saw*, a man cuts off his own foot with a dull hacksaw.

- In Stephen J. Cannell's new novel, *Cold Hit*, someone shoots homeless men in the head, cuts off their fingers, and carves runic symbols in their chests.

You may believe that you've already gotten a bellyful of Hollywood violence, from *Psycho* to *Pulp Fiction*. But many pop culture experts agree that the lavish intensity of today's carnage makes previous eras look dainty.

The Visceral Path

"In the last few years, there's been a steady increase in the amplitude," said Stephen Prince, a professor of communication studies at Virginia Tech and the president of the international Society for Cinema and Media Studies. "Characters were beheaded in D.W. Griffith's [silent movie] *Intolerance* in 1916, but it was shown quickly and in long shot.

"Today you might see it in slow motion, with close-ups from multiple camera setups. It'll have an aggressive sound component to make it texturized and sensual. You'll hear the arterial blood splatter. The whole treatment is much more detailed and loving."

Novels are going down the same visceral path.

"I have noticed an increase in gratuitous violence, a desensitizing of violence," wrote Oline Cogdill, the longtime mysteries columnist for the South Florida *Sun-Sentinel*, in an e-mail.

". . . Some writers feel because films and television have gone so far, that they need to do that to attract an audience."

"In the old days of the thriller/mystery, murder was the ultimate crime but it was usually just murder," concurred Margaret Cannon, a critic for the Toronto *Globe and Mail*, by e-mail. "Now we have . . . sexual crimes, torture, really nasty stuff, along with the murder."

The ratcheting up of violence is most evident in this season's network TV series.

"With competition from cable, I think networks have had to go further in graphic representations of violence," said Cynthia Felando, a film-studies lecturer at the University of California, Santa Barbara. "I've had squeamish reactions watching *CSI*."

Television's top-rated show has certainly had its stomach-turning moments, such as last season's buried-alive finale directed by [*Pulp Fiction* film director] Quentin Tarantino, or the recent episode in which human remains were found grossly decomposed in a steamy car trunk.

But CBS's Vegas crime-scene geeks have plenty of company. In the debut of the network's new drama *Criminal Minds*, for instance, a woman—bound, gagged and caged—frantically struggles as her rapist/serial-killer captor jabs at her bloody fingertips with pincers.

Why are TV producers suddenly so enamored of hard-core gore? They may be sublimating their frustrated sex drive.

"In the post-Janet Jackson media environment, the networks and TV producers and writers are wary of pushing the content envelope as aggressively as they have with regard to sexual content," said Melissa Caldwell, director of research for the Parents Television Council, a watchdog group. ". . . As the law stands now, the (Federal Communications Commission) has no authority over violent content." . . .

Until now, politicians have focused most of their rhetoric and concern about media violence on video games, because of their youth appeal. In this era of an Xbox in every kid's bedroom, these kill-'em-all games have set a new standard for graphic and casually cruel violence.

Combine that with increasingly cutthroat movies, DVDs and TV shows, and it's clear that today's young people are being exposed to unprecedented levels of violence.

Engendering Fear

What effect does all this savagery have on the audience?

"It makes all of us fearful," said Scott Poland, a psychology professor at Nova Southeastern University. As administrator of a national task force, he has responded to 11 school shooting incidents, from Columbine to Red Lake, Minn. "We'd all like to believe that man is basically good, but with all the crime and violence depicted, it gets harder and harder to hold onto that viewpoint."

Are TV shows creating a climate of fear, or are they reflecting one that already exists?

"Today's television audiences have witnessed . . . the events surrounding 9/11, the wars in Afghanistan and Iraq, the Oklahoma City bombing and a myriad of natural disasters," wrote Charlton McIlwain, an assistant professor in New York University's Department of Culture and Communication, in an e-mail.

"We've seen the . . . real carnage inflicted on the victims of such violence. And because of the seemingly daily communication of terror threats, we're constantly reminded that we ourselves may be next."

One of the popular media's glaring distortions is its grossly exaggerated incidence of serial killing. If you judge by books, TV and movies, approximately one out of every three people is a budding Ted Bundy [notorious serial killer]. The fiends figure prominently in prime-time shows from CBS's *Cold Case* to ABC's *Night Stalker*, and in a coming two-part crossover episode of the "NY" and "Miami" franchises of *CSI*.

"That scares the hell out of us—the idea of being killed randomly by someone we don't even know," Poland said. "That doesn't fit the real pattern of violence in America where serial killers are exceedingly rare. But it sells books." . . .

Pushing Violence Further

The TV and film industries are self-governed through content-ratings systems. And those classifications tend to be vague and inconsistent.

"It's important for people to realize that ratings have 'crept' over time," said Kimberly Thompson, director of the KidsRisk Project at Harvard University's School of Public Health. "Looking at films over an 11-year period, we showed that ratings crept so much they moved almost a full category. Today's PG-13 movie is like an R-rated film from 10 years ago."

Many film historians hold that serious directors are immune to the siren song of violence.

"Look at the box office top 10 last year (in which the only big money maker that drew an R-rating for its reliance on graphic gore was *The Passion of the Christ*—very much a special case)," wrote Michael Medved, film critic and nationally syndicated radio host, in an e-mail. "This year the most obnoxiously sadistic films—*The Devil's Rejects* and the just released *Domino*—both opened to lukewarm . . . business."

But that misses the point. Obviously lurid movies such as *The Devil's Rejects* aren't "date films." However, they enjoy healthy afterlives.

More and more Hollywood projects are based on hard-core source materials.

"We are in a cycle . . . during which horror films, particularly violent movies like *Saw*, are selling unusually well on home video," wrote Scott Hettrick, editor of the trade magazine *DVD Exclusive*, by e-mail.

Saw has earned more than $90 million so far on video, nearly 65 percent more than it took in at the U.S. box office.

And more and more Hollywood projects are based on hard-core source materials. The films *Sin City* and *A History of Violence*, both critically lauded, were adapted from gritty graphic novels. The *Resident Evil* films and the current *Doom* are re-creations of violent video games. Other movies, such as *Dawn of the Dead*, with its incessant skull-splattering kill shots, just look like first-person-shooter games.

How far will this trend toward ultraviolence go? The only logical answer is "further." Once artistic boundaries of taste or restraint have been crossed, they are rarely reinstated. The demons will not go back in the bottle.

We may have to resign ourselves to the entertainment climate described by Mandy Patinkin's character in a recent episode of *Criminal Minds*: "Finding new ways to hurt each other is what we're good at."

7

Violent Video Games Teach Children How to Kill

Bill France

Bill France is a child advocate in the criminal justice system and has worked as director of clinical programs at Luther Child Center in Everett, Washington.

Violent video games are instructional simulations that show young players how to kill efficiently and without feeling. By treating the animated victims as mere fodder for the player's killing spree, young people become desensitized to the act of murder and its consequences. In effect, players of violent video games are learning the uncaring and dehumanizing attitudes displayed by some of society's most grisly serial killers. To counteract the potential dangers of video violence, parents need to oversee the types of games their children play.

The question is how to alert parents to the dangers hiding in their children's video games without sounding like just another voice on a broken old record.

The broken record would be about violence, and it would seem that the warnings have all been issued.

But, try these three points for starters:

- If a parent wanted their children to develop attitudes like [Seattle's] Gary Ridgway, the confessed killer of at least 48 women, these games might provide a good training ground.

Bill France, "Violent Video Games Are Training Children to Kill," *Daily Herald* www.heraldnet.com, November 18, 2003. Copyright © 2003 The Daily Herald Col., Everett, Wash. Reproduced by permission of the author.

- These video games are not spectator activities, like going to a violent movie. They use simulation techniques that are used to teach people to fly a plane, drive a car or fight wars.

- Parents cannot trust their neighborhood stores to not sell hyper-violent video games to young children.

Sound desperate? If so, take a look at the new video by Mothers Against Violence in America. It is part of its "Campaign for a Game Smart Community," and asks, "Do you know what video games your children are playing?"

The Mothers Against Violence video even upsets professionals who are used to working with violence. For example, Janice Ellis, Snohomish County prosecutor, and Bruce Eklund, assistant administrator of the Snohomish County Juvenile Court, brought the group's video to my attention. Both were dismayed with game-based human behavior that transcends mere violence.

[Violent video games] make victims into something much less than human.

Killing Without Remorse

But, take the three concerns one at a time.

First, people were thoroughly chilled by confessed serial killer Ridgway's admissions and descriptions [of his murders, as he related them to prosecutors in 2003 when he agreed to provide details in a bargain that spared him the death penalty].

Even the sanitized details within the King County prosecutor's summary are so bad that the cover page warns that the report ". . . contains graphic and disturbing descriptions," which may not be suitable for every reader.

Ridgway remembers where he dumped bodies, how he planned his killings and tricked people into his traps, the descriptions of his many cars, and the floor plans of his several homes. He doesn't remember the faces or names of the 48 victims he admitted killing.

In his words, "Like I said, they didn't mean anything to me."

He killed only women. He killed no men, he said, "'cause they didn't give no sexual gratification to me."

And, this is largely what some well-known video games do. Make victims into something much less than human. They are killed. Their heads are cut off and blood spurts from their necks.

The dead bodies are kicked and urinated on. The killer laughs at them and makes crude sexual comments. Sex and violence weave into deadly behaviors, over and over.

The video game scripts could be culled from Gary Ridgway's confession.

Simulating the Act of Killing

Second, these games are not movies. Nor are they spectator games. Rather, they are simulations.

The games use techniques known to be effective in teaching young people to drive cars or go to war. Simulation, Eklund points out, is designed to hone the trainee's instincts, to help them build habits that they can carry out quickly, without second thoughts.

Video games laced with human atrocities help young, impressionable people practice killing without care.

The youngsters who hold the joysticks and sit at the keyboards hold the guns and axes. Young players practice cutting heads off. They rehearse shooting police officers and urinating on them.

It is worth stating again. Every time a youngster plays one of these games, parents, they are in simulation. They practice self-talk, saying things to dehumanize their victims. They practice laughing at others' pain and justifying murder. They use words to humiliate others and see how dehumanizing acts feel.

Violent Games Are Easy to Obtain

Third, the Mothers Against Violence group sent underage youngsters into familiar stores, and 15 out of 17 of the stores sold adult games to children under 12.

Actually, it is disturbing that these games excite some adults, but the rating system might manage the damage better than selling every game to every age. But, the ratings do no good if retailers don't honor them.

As always, this means parents and other caring adults have to be the last line of defense for children in their own care. And, in the overwhelming number of cases in which parents protect, nurture and guide their children, their actions work.

One danger for children lies in any tendency of parents to think "not my child."

Before drawing that conclusion they should consider four facts.

- Video games are expected to reach $20 billion in sales this year. That is a sizable piece of the growing economy everybody is hoping for, and it works directly against what most parents want for their children.

- Every year, enough video games are sold to put two of them in every American household.

- More than nine of every 10 American children play video games.

- Research shows that playing violent video games increases children's violent thoughts and aggressive behaviors.

The first, last and best line of defense for most children is their parents. On the other hand, children whose parents do not defend them are more influenced by video games than are other children. Children who are protected by their parents are growing up with children who are not.

So parents have to first protect and nurture their own children, but it helps when they also help protect and nurture other children.

I won't name the most violent video games because I won't advertise them. Violent video games need only change their names or move the violence into other games. Children just need for their parents to play their video games with them.

8

Violent Video Games Improve Learning and Cognition Skills

Douglas A. Gentile and J. Ronald Gentile

Douglas A. Gentile is an assistant professor of psychology and Research Fellow at the Institute of Science and Society at Iowa State University in Ames. He is also director of research for the National Institute on Media and the Family. J. Ronald Gentile is an emeritus professor of educational psychology at the State University of New York at Buffalo.

Violent video games are exemplary teachers of cognitive skills and learning principles. Such games typically modify game play to suit the skill of the players, allowing the players to challenge themselves with varying degrees of difficulty. Mastering the requirements of each skill level encourages players by building self-esteem through a sense of accomplishment and competence. In addition, through the repetition needed to master a specific level of game play, players reinforce cognitive and learning skills—such as memory and problem solving—that eventually ensure success. Such skills are not limited to game play and can be transferred to other areas of learning, benefiting young people in academic development.

Although the research has become clearer that violent video games can cause people to have more aggressive thoughts, feelings, and behaviors, our goal here is to praise video games

Douglas A. Gentile and J. Ronald Gentile, "Excerpts," *Violent Video Games as Exemplary Teachers,* paper presented at the biennial meeting of the Society for Research in Child Development, April 9, 2005, pp. 3, 4, 5, 6. Reproduced by permission of the authors.

for their effective use of psychological principles of learning, cognition, and instruction. Video games are excellent teachers along several dimensions.

Reaching Objectives and Mastering Skills

First, the games have clear objectives, often set at multiple difficulty levels to adapt to the prior knowledge and skills of each learner. Second, and related to the first, the pace of the activities can be adjusted for faster or slower learners, novices or experts, to truly deliver differentiated instruction. Inventing ways of matching objectives and pace to the capabilities of learners is no small accomplishment. . . . Moreover, there is empirical evidence for many memory tasks that the average learning rate of the top third of any class is at least three times faster than the bottom third, with the fastest and slowest learners in the same class differing by even larger multiples.

Third, learning is active with practice, feedback, and more practice to the point of mastery. This is in contrast to much classroom learning in which teachers lecture on or demonstrate a concept or skill, then take questions, if any, and move on to cover other material. But as is well known in the development of skills such as sports or music, learners have questions only after attempting to *do* what was demonstrated. Feedback and corrections operate only then, which in classrooms often happens only much later (e.g., on a unit test) and thus is too late to be of much help. Practice to the point of mastery—that is, to a higher rather than lower standard of accuracy—is predictive of how much is remembered later, as well as how much savings will occur in relearning at a later date.

Overlearning and Self-Esteem Building

Fourth, once mastered, the knowledge and skills are practiced further to provide *overlearning*. This helps the knowledge and skills become automatized and consolidated in memory, so that the learner can begin to focus consciously on comprehending or applying new information. In other words, the novice is beginning to process and organize new information with more expertise. [B.S.] Bloom (1986) illustrated this process for developing reading ability. Only after knowledge of letters and sounds are automatized can the budding reader recognize whole words. Only after achieving a number of "sight words" can the reader focus on the meaning of the sentences.

Fifth, mastery of an objective is reinforced both extrinsically (with points, totals, better weapons, more money, more health, etc.) and intrinsically (by advancement to higher levels of complexity and the self-esteem that accompanies increased competence). This last point is perhaps underappreciated by educators who have been told to praise often so as to increase children's self-esteem. But a wide range of theorists agree that perceived self-efficacy arises from competence or efficacy, and lack of competence leads to learned helplessness. Likewise, mastering the essential tasks of school results in solving the identity crisis of that age ("I am what I can do"), while non-mastery leads to feelings of inferiority. . . .

Sixth, and related to the fifth, video games are well-sequenced in levels of increasing difficulty, complexity or pace, with success at subsequent levels contingent upon competencies mastered at previous levels. Consider the example of the popular first-person-shooter game *Halo*. For the first hour of play, the game not only sets up the story (you are a warrior in a science fiction future, in which you are saving humans from attacking aliens), but also teaches you how to play. The game characters and spaceship computer teach you systematically which control buttons to use to look around, to walk, to crouch, to jump, to pick up weapons, to reload, etc. This is necessary partly because of the complexity of the game controller (13 buttons, joysticks, pads, and triggers). But after teaching a specific skill, the game immediately gives you a chance to practice it. The game then gives immediate feedback, including adapting to your specific skill using the controller. For example, the first author had difficulty with the joystick in looking up and down—it was more "natural" to pull back to look up and push forward to look down (as one would in an airplane). This was contrary to the default settings on the game. The game noticed this, and inverted the joystick controls to fit the author's predilection, and asked if this was better. Over the course of the first hour of play, a series of skills are taught systematically, with feedback and opportunities for practice, until one has learned several skills necessary for successful game play (such as how to use the information shown on the display, when to reload, and how to sneak up behind one's prey for silent kills).

This is the embodiment of the *spiral curriculum*, in which each learning objective has identifiable prerequisites which, when mastered, facilitate transfer to the next level of difficulty. Thus, learners come to see mastery of an objective not as the completion of a learning objective, or "benchmark" in current educational lingo. Rather, mastery is properly conceived as the beginning: you are now ready to use that knowledge or skill in some meaningful way on the road toward expertise.

Each subsequent encounter with [a] game provides . . . memory benefits.

Memory Skills and Problem Solving

Seventh, because video games are adaptable in level of difficulty and pace, they encourage a close-to-optimal combination of massed and distributed practice. Initial attempts at the game, no matter how abysmal, receive feedback or a score immediately and few can resist trying again and again until they begin to show progress. Such massed practice eventually begins to produce diminishing returns (when a plateau is reached or fatigue sets in). However, the repetition has begun to develop both physical and mental skills and habits (e.g., eye-hand coordination, knowledge of what is required, etc.) on parts of the task, but always in the context of the whole sequence. Each subsequent encounter with the game provides the memory benefits of distributed practice—namely, relearning anything that was forgotten; providing new cues for memory, interpreting new information or examples with what is already in memory and reorganizing the memory accordingly. This combination of massed practice to build sufficient initial mastery to play the game, followed by distributed practice over days or weeks to prevent forgetting is optimal for the development of automatized structures of knowledge, or schemas.

Eighth, knowledge or skills learned and practiced in multiple ways, on several problems, or in a variety of contexts are more likely to transfer than when practiced in only one way on a single kind of problem, or the same context. One reason for this, in [J.D.] Bransford, [A.L.] Brown, and [R.R.] Cocking's words, is that "with multiple contexts, students are more likely to abstract the relevant features of concepts and develop a more flexible representation of knowledge" (1999). Multiple contexts also provide a variety of cues for recall rather than memory having to rely on availability of cues from the original context or problem situation. . . .

Multiple ways of solving problems or performing skills also avoid the mental sets or rigidities that naturally arise from success with a particular method. To avoid the aversion so many Americans have to the metric system, for example, students need to learn to measure in multiple ways—feet and meters, pounds and grams—and then practice using them in math, science, and social problems in school and in the rest of life. Learning multiple ways of representing division of fractions, rather than simply memorizing the "invert and multiply" algorithm is more likely to lead to greater comprehension than the same amount of time spent simply practicing the algorithm. Violent video games are set in many contexts. Some are set in historical times, some are modern, some are very realistic, some are cartoonish, some are futuristic, etc. Some portray hand-to-hand combat, some use small arms, some use military weapons, some use laser guns, and one popular game even uses a golf club as a lethal weapon. The common feature among all of these different games and contexts is that violence is the solution to whatever problem the gamer/student faces. This is exactly the best way to teach so that the student will be able to transfer the underlying concept to new situations.

Provocative scenes of . . . violence . . . supply vivid visual images, which are known to create better memory than the same information provided verbally.

Compelling Images Aid Learning

In addition to the above well-known principles of educational instruction, video game producers also use time-honored "tricks" that have been well-known by the media and advertisers. For example, [R.] Kubey & [M.] Csikszentmihalyi (2002) describe how the "orienting response," first described by Ivan Pavlov, has been used to increase attention to television ads. Visual or auditory changes, such as edits that change the angle of camera view or sound effects, make us look at them. Increasing the frequency of edits has been shown to improve recognition memory (up to a point . . . there is an optimal level). Furthermore, provocative scenes of sex and violence not only capture one's attention, but also supply vivid visual images, which are known to create better memory than the same information provided verbally. Active participation in aggressive or provocative scenes in video games increases physiological arousal. This physiological responding in the context of "playing fun games" is likely to condition one's emotions to such activities, not unlike other addictive "highs." Indeed, there is some research demonstrating that the brain releases dopamine in response to playing violent video games. Dopaminergic neurotransmission may also be involved in learning, reinforcement of behavior, attention, and sensorimotor integration as well. Because the difficulty of the games, which varies as one progresses, guarantees that reinforcement will be intermittent, not continuous, they take full advantage of the addictive nature of intermittent reinforcement (e.g., slot machines). While research in this area is still young, there is evidence that video games may indeed be "addictive" for some people, perhaps as many as 15% to 20% of players.

Finally, these games are marketed widely as something everyone must have, thus making skill in such games an important social currency for popularity among children (especially among boys).

9

Violence in Rap Music Is a Serious Problem

Al Sharpton

The Reverend Al Sharpton is a clergyman and social activist. In the late 1960s Sharpton began working in the civil rights movement. He fought mainly against drug abuse and other community problems in New York's inner-city African American neighborhoods. In 1991, Sharpton founded the civil rights organization National Action Network, Inc., and continues to serve as its president. He has campaigned to win several state and federal posts including a seat in the U.S Senate (1992 and 1994), the office of New York City mayor (1997), and the office of president of the United States (2004). He failed to win any of his election bids.

Rap and hip hop culture is vibrant, and its artists have appealing stories to tell. However, part of the rap artist's image is based on boasting and the threat of violence to back up any verbal challenges. Occasionally a war of words between feuding rap stars turns into real violence and murder. One such feud claimed the lives of rap legends Tupac Shakur and Biggie Smalls. Unfortunately, record labels do nothing to defuse the atmosphere of violence because it sells more records. The federal government, then, must take action against labels and artists who promote hostility. Namely, the Federal Communications Commission should impose sanctions against rap performers and their labels if either is connected to incidents of real violence.

Al Sharpton, "I Don't Hate the Game, I Question the Players," *Billboard*, vol. 117, April 9, 2005, p. 12. Copyright 2005 Billboard, property of VNU Media, Inc. Reproduced by permission of the author.

Hip-hop beefs are about as old as hip-hop itself. Lately, the tone, intensity and seriousness of these conflicts have created an environment that is entirely too permissive of violence. The role that radio, TV and other media have in creating these conflicts must be examined by the entire music community, because the violence must be attacked and eradicated.

Let me be clear right up front, I am not attempting in any way to infringe upon the rights of what any artist is able to say in their creations. I do not advocate any type of censorship. My fundamental goal is to create an environment where the myriad of companies that benefit from the success of hip-hop feel a true sense of responsibility to the young Americans who love and support the music.

Taking Responsibility

How come record labels do not have social responsibility officers? The short answer is, they do not care. The labels hide behind the expansive protection of the First Amendment without accepting the responsibility of being citizens of this great nation. As we all know, [in March 2005] a gun battle ensued after a series of on-air interviews on New York's Hot 97. A verbal fracas between Interscope labelmates 50 Cent and the Game escalated to the point where a member of the Game's entourage ended up being shot.

I don't hate the game . . . I question the players.

At the point when artists' imagery created on wax spills into the streets for real, their protections as artists must stop. Record labels that cleverly engender much of the dangerous and sullen imagery for the promotion of these artists have to take responsibility for the ultimate reality shows they have created. Orchestrated makeup sessions and giving checks to charity are simply not enough to make up for the culture of violence and the mind-set that this type of behavior foists on our communities.

Right now, 50 Cent and the Game collectively hold four, FOUR of the top eight songs on the Billboard Hot 100 Airplay chart. I am not begrudging these young men their success, but I do wish to call into question a system that possibly rewards behavior that we are working every day to remove from our communities.

I don't hate the game . . . I question the players.

Conflict and Drama Equal More Sales

I am especially concerned about the hip-hop recording industry, because they have been here before. Several years ago, what started as a war of words between hip-hop executives on opposite coasts culminated with the untimely and violent deaths of Tupac Shakur and Christopher Wallace [aka Biggie Smalls]. You see, we have seen this movie before: Hip-hop artists engage in verbal jousting, their battles move to wax, wax goes to interviews on radio and TV, then more wax, more beef . . . until some type of violent conclusion occurs.

The collective ego of hip-hop requires—almost demands— that confrontations escalate, oftentimes to violence.

Tupac and Big, Nas and Jay-Z, Ja Rule and 50 [Cent], Eminem and the Source, 50 and the hip-hop nation. Beef, conflict, drama . . . more sales.

I am asking the Federal Communications Commission [FCC] to take an active role in curtailing an environment of violence. I wish to see it enact a 90-day ban on any artist, or known affiliate, who engages in any type of violence in our communities. This ban should include all radio and video airplay. No MTV. No BET. No Clear Channel. No Radio One. No Emmis.

I recently met in Washington, D.C., with the new FCC chairman and two executives. I know the FCC does not regulate satellite radio, magazines or the Internet; I would ask those entities to comply as well.

Furthermore, if there are successive violations, I am requesting that the penalties escalate. I would ask for the formation of a commission of executives in the music, radio and TV business to intelligently deliberate and render opinions on which companies or artists have crossed the line regarding violence.

During the past year, we have seen the vigilance the FCC displayed in protecting the nation's airwaves because of an untimely "wardrobe malfunction." Now, outside of our nation's radio stations we have a situation where "humanity malfunctions" routinely occur.

The incident [in March 2005 at Hot 97] was not the first; Lil' Kim is facing real jail time for being present at a similar gun battle that took place in 2001. There was a confrontation at a radio station in Detroit. Countless other conflicts have developed as a result of on-air braggadocio and challenges.

An End to the Violence

I am not trying to stop the verbal jousting and banter that is endemic in hip-hop, but I will use all of my resources to ask the industry to stand with me and partner with the National Action Network to demand a cessation of all forms of violent interactions.

I will not stop with the FCC; I will aggressively seek to gain stock positions in the companies that are the stakeholders in all of this game of violence for profit. Many record companies are privately held or listed on foreign exchanges. But many of our nation's radio and video outlets are publicly listed companies. I will also seek to engage companies like Reebok that enjoy a successful marketing relationship with hip-hop artists.

To be clear, my goal is not to keep these artists from enjoying the fruits of their artistry. My goal is to demand that all who profit from their artistry take responsibility for a zero-tolerance policy toward violence. I will not stop.

I love hip-hop. I am often conflicted by its message and imagery, but I love its spirit. I do not concur with its wanton misogyny or nihilism, but I love its ability to tell stories.

The energy and creativity of hip-hop are reminiscent of what I have come to love about the fight for civil rights. Hip-hop is urgent, demanding and oftentimes tells a story we all do not want to hear.

But like hip-hop, I too have a story to tell. Violence must stop now . . . I thought I told you that I won't stop.

10

Rap Music is Not to Blame for Violence

Free Lance-Star

The Free Lance-Star *is a local paper serving Fredericksburg, Virginia.*

Rap music is often criticized for its violent content. However, the whole genre is not to blame for the words or actions of some rap artists. After all, there are many socially conscious performers who put forth a positive message. Unfortunately, the nastiest rap songs are often the most popular, but this has more to do with the influence of the entertainment industry than with listeners' relationship to the music. Critics must also stop blaming music for real world acts of violence; individuals, not a musical style or song, have to be held responsible for their own actions.

Rap and violence—two terms that are, to many people, synonymous.

Critics believe that the lyrics of modern rap songs have something to do with the violence. Early hip-hop provided individuals with an avenue to express themselves. Modern rap centers around bling, money, cars, and other materialistic things.

Modern rap also has a history of degrading women.

Can we really link rap music to violence? Or should we blame the violence on individuals? Our society is drawn to negative things, after all. People would rather watch sex, violence, and guns instead of programs that promote good morals.

Free Lance-Star, "Blame Individuals for Their Actions—Not a Song or Genre," February 5, 2006. Copyright 2006, The Free Lance-Star Publishing Co. of Fredericksburg, VA. Reproduced by permission.

Role Models for the Underclass

I believe individuals should be held accountable for their actions. For example: I can listen to music and not be affected by it—because I know how to filter in the good with the bad. But individuals who do not have good ethics will have a harder time processing information.

I wish more rappers would understand that they are looked upon as role models. How they talk, walk, and dress becomes the hot topic among teenagers.

Just think about this—the same person who glorifies guns, degrades women, and promotes promiscuous behavior is your child's role model.

It's shocking that the nastiest songs dominate the Billboard charts. People like Martin Luther King, William Shakespeare, and many more are being replaced in the popular culture by 50 Cent, Ludacris, and others.

The reality is that underclass African-Americans find it difficult to identify with historical figures.

It's all part of being a product of your environment.

The recent tragedy in Fredericksburg—when a young man was killed while a song blared out violent lyrics—only adds fuel to the cultural fire.

Rap-related violence affects other countries as well—most notably England and Canada. London and Toronto have experienced gun-related crimes due to turf wars between rival gangs (centered around rap music). The gangster rap that dominated the 1980s and '90s has pretty much diminished, but the gangs are still prevalent.

Positive Rap

So rap has attained a negative stigma—but not all of it is bad. An alternative to the commercial rap that dominates the airwaves and radio would be "conscious rap."

Conscious rappers are usually more aware of their surroundings. They speak on political issues, social issues, and issues that plague our youth. The pioneers of hip-hop (Rakim, KRS-1, Kurtis Blow, etc.) promoted social awareness and delivered their messages with a cause.

Another route would be "Christian rap," which is self-explanatory.

I still believe that individuals, not the music . . . , bear responsibility for violence.

Some parents believe that buying an edited CD will be effective, but I disagree. They could expose their children to other genres of music as well. People like Kenny Chesney, Keith Urban, U2, and countless others are great songwriters who incorporate good morals into their songs.

During adolescence, the pressure of being cool outweighs the concept of self—and it is our role to teach adolescents the importance of self identity.

I still believe that individuals, not the music in itself, bear responsibility for violence. For example, "crunk music" can be defined as music that incites the crowd. DJs may choose to play a crunk track because it is intended to liven up a party.

Now, does this rambunctious behavior lead to violence? The answer is yes and no. A responsible person would not follow the flock per se. You can party with common sense.

Blame Corporate America as Well

When tragedies happen, people point to the stereotypes. We should focus on why this happened, not who or what caused it. If you are going to blame rap music, then you should blame corporate America as well. Think about it—rap music sells the most, you can hear hip-hop elements in commercials, movies, cartoons, everywhere. How did this happen? People are driven by money.

The machine controls rap music nowadays, and we have to fight it and promote social awareness.

11

The Entertainment Industry Is Marketing Violence to Children

Daphne White

Daphne White is the executive director of the Lion & Lamb Project, a national grassroots collective of parents concerned about the marketing of violence to children. The organization provides information to parents on how to protect children from violent entertainment. It also lobbies industry executives and legislators to bring about changes in marketing violence to children.

The music, movie, and video game industries are marketing violent entertainment products to children. While these industries have all vowed to self-censor their product placement, none has made significant improvement in keeping violent content away from America's young people. Indeed, some are aggressively promoting violence to children. The video game industry, for example, often advertises mature-themed games in magazines and other venues aimed at children. Likewise, the movie industry often previews R-rated films during PG-rated shows. Because these industries have shown an unwillingness to bring about real change, parents and legislators will have to compel some compliance through laws devised to stop such immoral marketing.

I am speaking to you today as a mother of a 13-year-old boy, and as a former journalist who spent 20 years writing about education and family issues. I became concerned about

Daphne White, "Testimony presented to the House Subcommittee on Telecommunications and the Internet," July 20, 2001. Reproduced by permission of the author.

media violence when my son was two years old, and I noticed that violence was being marketed even to toddlers. I left journalism and became an activist when I learned that violent media images have been shown to have *lasting negative effects* on the attitude and behavior of children, and especially young children under the age of 8.

I am here representing millions of parents who want to tell the entertainment industry what that news anchorman shouted in the movie *Network*: "I'm mad as hell and I'm not going to take it anymore!"

We are here today to examine the entertainment industry's efforts to curb children's exposure to violent content, and specifically their efforts at reform since the Federal Trade Commission (FTC) report came out in September 2000.

Our children are . . . exposed to violent "entertainment" every single day.

In its September report, the FTC found that the video game, movie and music industries were indeed marketing adult-level violence to children in a "pervasive and aggressive" way. . . .

The FTC found, among other things, that children as young as nine years old were being used in focus groups to test R-rated movies; that internal marketing plans for R-rated movies and M-rated video games admitted that teens were the real audience for these adult-rated products; and that R-rated movies were being advertised directly to children in camps and at Boys and Girls Clubs.

I am sure the industry representatives assembled here today will tell you that all these practices have now stopped, that violence is no longer marketed to children, and that government need do nothing else to protect America's children.

Nothing could be further from the truth! As a parent, I can tell you that our children are still exposed to violent "entertainment" *every single day.*

Public Health Concern

It is important to understand that "entertainment" violence is neither innocuous nor harmless. On July 26, 2000, representatives of six public health organizations presented a Joint Letter to the Congress on this very topic.

"The conclusion of the public health community, based on over 30 years of research, is that viewing entertainment violence can lead to increases in aggressive attitudes, values and behavior, particularly in children," according [to] the statement. It was signed by the American Medical Association, the American Academy of Pediatrics, the American Psychological Association, the American Academy of Child & Adolescent Psychiatry, the American Psychiatric Association and the American Academy of Family Physicians.

If any of you work with the scientific community, you know how hard it is to get six organizations to agree to *anything.* While the entertainment industry pays its own consultants to debunk this research, I want to make it clear that the scientific *consensus* is clear: numerous studies "point overwhelmingly to a causal connection between media violence and aggressive behavior in some children," according to the public health groups.

In fact, while most of the long-term research focused on television violence—which is a passive *viewing* of violence—preliminary studies indicate that the negative impact of interactive violence may be "significantly more severe than that wrought by television, movies or music," according to the Joint Statement.

Because of the public health implications of this issue, the Senate asked the FTC for a follow-up report, released in April [2001], to assess how much progress had been made by industry since September. In that second report, the FTC did found that the movie and video game industries have made "*some*" progress, but the music industry has been made *none*. Much work remained to be done by all three industries. As a parents' organization, we would agree with that assessment. . . .

Video Violence for Everyone

Let me give you some examples of the types of marketing that is still taking place today, 10 months after the original Federal Trade Commission report came out. Let's start with the video game industry, as this industry claims to have done the best job in reforming its practices.

Here is a recent Toys R Us circular—Toys R Us, let us remember, is a toy store. It sells toys to children. But here is an ad showing a young boy surrounded by Game Boys—the platform geared most specifically to children—and a variety of video games. This looks like a child-friendly page, and features an array of 14 games including *Donkey Kong*, *Frogger* and *Scooby Doo*. (These games are all rated "E" for Everyone by the industry ratings group the Entertainment Software Review Board, or ESRB.)

But a closer look shows that snuck in among the many children's games rated "E" on this page are two very adult games: *Perfect Dark* and *Conker's Bad Fur Day*, both rated "M" for mature. Children, as well as their parents, will likely conclude that *all* the games on this Toys R Us circular page are appropriate for youth.

Why is [a] game about a "hung-over, foulmouthed squirrel" . . . coming out in an "E"-rated version for the Game Boy?

They would be wrong, of course. Here is one section from a *New York Times* review of *Perfect Dark*: "Swarms of deadly enemies must be eliminated . . . shooting accurately at bad guys takes enormous amounts of practice . . . Practice pays off . . . and yes, blood splatters the walls and floors behind and beneath enemies on the receiving end of your arsenal."

Perfect Dark is a Nintendo game that looks and feels like an older game called *Goldeneye 007.* The James Bond–based *Goldeneye*—one of the most violent first-person shooter games I have ever seen—was somehow rated "T" for Teen, and was very popular with teens. While *Perfect Dark* is now rated "M" for Mature, placing an ad for this game in the midst of kids' titles is clearly an effort to target market this adult game to children. . . .

Conker's Bad Fur Day is also rated "M" for Mature. According to Nintendo, this risqué game is purely an entry for adults. So why are they advertising the game in a Toys R Us catalogue? And why is this game about a "hung-over, foul-mouthed squirrel" (in the words of the *Village Voice*) coming out in an "E"-rated version for the Game Boy?? . . .

These are just some examples of how the video game industry markets violent games to children. The Interactive Digital Software Association, the industry trade association, has so far refused to adopt the three very *reasonable* and *modest* recommendations for reform proposed in the September FTC report. As a result, the April follow-up FTC report found that most video game companies are still advertising adult-rated video games in magazines with a large under-17 audience.

We agree with the FTC finding that the video industry can do much more than it is now doing to stop the marketing of violence to children. But I also agree with IDSA [Interactive Digital Software Association] President Doug Lowenstein on one point. In his address to the annual industry trade show E3, the Electronic Entertainment Expo, Mr. Lowenstein noted how video games are now ubiquitous in the home, in cars and vans, in military settings, on airplanes, on the Internet . . . and even in schools.

He described an interactive video game that is now being used in Willard Model Elementary School in Norfolk, VA. "It's just a matter of time before more and more games will be used as teaching tools," Mr. Lowenstein said. I agree that video games *can* and *are* used as teaching tools. The question, Mr. Lowenstein, is *what kinds* of lessons will video games teach our children in the future?

Will video game technology continue to teach children to feel *satisfaction* in snapping necks, running over pedestrians, blowing policemen to pieces, and eviscerating people? Or will this technology be used to teach values that most American parents feel comfortable with?

[Movie] studios are still advertising R-rated movies during television programs most popular with teens.

Mature Movies Previewed to Young Audiences

Now let's turn to the movie industry. Again, "some" progress has been made—but not nearly enough. This industry has also refused to accept the threshold recommendations for reform proposed in the FTC report.

True, R-rated previews—"appropriate for all audiences"—are no longer shown before G-rated matinees. But previews for R-rated features are still shown before PG-13 features, which are largely aimed at teens. And studios are still advertising R-rated movies during television programs most popular with teens.

Finally, the movie and television industries are still airing R-rated movies such as *Scream* during a time when many children are watching. In the case of *Scream* and *Scream 2*, which aired in January 2001, that time was 8 p.m. And just to make sure kids knew about this televised movie, Fox advertised the film during the after-school cartoon programs, when the greatest number of children are watching television.

I won't even *begin* to talk about how inappropriate the current movie rating system is—and how much violence is considered "appropriate" for PG-13, PG and even G-rated movies. But I can tell you that many parents are appalled at the scenes they see, with their children, when they take them to movies the industry assures them are "appropriate" for children.

The FTC recommends that each of the industries should "establish or expand codes that prohibit target marketing to children and impose sanctions for violations." So, what has the movie industry done? They came up with a 12-step plan poetically stating that R-rated films will not be "inappropriately specifically" targeted to children. *Inappropriately specifically?* That phrase alone would earn a D-minus in most high school writing classes.

We found the movie industry's 12-step plan so full of loopholes any mom could drive a mini-van through it. So after the second set of Senate hearings—in which each of the seven studio heads appeared to commit to slightly different "specific and inappropriate" reforms—we sent a simple, 14-question survey to all the studio heads who had testified.

As a parent group, we wanted to understand a few simple facts, such as:

- Will movie theaters continue to air previews for R-rated movies before PG-rated features?

- Will movie theaters advertise R-rated films on national television before 9 p.m.?

- Will movie theaters advertise R-rated movies on teen Internet sites?

- Does the effort to "not inappropriately specifically target children" mean a stop to the practice of licensing children's products such as toys, toy guns, action figures, fast-food promotions and other products based on R-rated movies?

Not one studio bothered to answer a single one of these questions. Meanwhile, the Motion Picture Association of America assures parents that their rating system and their 12-step program are there for the sole purpose of *helping* parents make wise choices. But in truth, when a parents' group such as ours asks for information, the movie industry can't come up with even "yes" or "no" answers to simple questions. . . .

If the video game industry is really so proud of its voluntary self-enforcement *system, they should be eager to display that system to parents.*

I would like to add that IDSA has been equally uncooperative in answering our questions. In the FTC's April report—which IDSA claims it passed with flying colors—the agency mentioned some new marketing and advertising policies the video game industry has adopted. When we requested those policies from the IDSA, our phone calls were not returned. We had to file a Freedom of Information Act request with the FTC to get the information. Eventually we received that information, after paying the FTC a fee. . . .

As a parents' group, we would like to know: *Where are the teeth??* What *specific* guidelines have video game companies adopted to stop the marketing of violence to children? And what sanctions do companies face if they don't comply with these *voluntary* guidelines?

We believe this information should be public. If the video game industry is really so proud of its *voluntary self-enforcement* system, they should be eager to display that system to parents and other concerned adults. Show us your voluntary system, and how you will enforce it. That way, parents will have more confidence in your industry. . . .

Business Interests vs. the Public Good

About the music industry: I won't say much beyond what my Russian grandmother would have said—their total and unequivocal *refusal* to reform their marketing system is "beneath contempt."

Like the movie and video game industries, the music industry likes to hide behind the fig leaf of the First Amendment. But as [Supreme Court] Justice Potter Stewart once said, "You are all confused about what you have a right to do under the Constitution and *the right thing to do.*"

I am a mother, not a constitutional lawyer. But I would like to quote former Federal Communications Commission chair Newton Minow, who wrote: "It would surely come as a surprise to those who wrote the First Amendment to see that Americans now cite it not to begin discussion of the public interest, but as a reason to *close* it."

Let's get real here: These three entertainment industries are not *really* in the business of protecting the First Amendment. They are in the business of promoting their members' bottom line. But at what cost? I am here to tell you, as a mother, that this cost involves our children's lives.

To quote Newton Minow once again, "The First Amendment is considered a 'preferred freedom'—one that, when balanced against other rights, gets the benefit of the doubt—but it is not an absolute freedom. It cannot be exercised at the expense of other constitutional rights or, in narrowly defined categories, contrary to public safety or well-being."

The First Amendment is being used by industry ... to close *debate, not to* open *debate.*

The First Amendment was designed for political speech: Until very recently, commercial speech was *not* accorded nearly the same rights as political speech. Likewise, the First Amendment has allowed for the protection of children; for example, it is no longer legal to advertise alcohol, or cigarettes, or pornography to children. Corporations can no longer argue that restricting the marketing of those products has rung a death knell for the First Amendment.

I ask you today, as the Representatives of parents across the country, to broaden your thinking about the First Amendment, and the protection that should be accorded children under this Amendment.

I also urge you to consider holding a separate set of congressional hearings on these First Amendment issues, so a real *debate* about this amendment can take place. Right now, I'm afraid, the First Amendment is being used by industry as the first and best tool to *close* debate, not to *open* debate.

America's parents—America's children—*deserve better marketing, and better entertainment.*

The Need for Enforcement

In conclusion, I would like to as the members of this subcommittee to consider follow-up actions to today's oversight hearing. All manner of violence is *still* being marketed to children, as I have demonstrated. The First Amendment is *not* an excuse to do nothing—it is a challenge to do *more* to protect the freedom of parents and children alike. Freedom to live in a peaceful, nonviolent, and civil society.

I also ask the three industries represented here today to clean up their marketing practices toward children, voluntarily adopt the FTC recommendations, and set up stringent, *transparent* and enforceable self-regulatory provisions to stop the types of marketing efforts discussed here.

If the industries fail to adopt these standards voluntarily, I ask this subcommittee to consider putting legislative teeth behind the FTC recommendations.

America's parents—America's *children*—deserve better marketing, and better entertainment, than we are getting. Parents should not be forced by these media companies to become policemen and women in their our homes—to constantly say "no!" to our children when it comes to movies and music and video games.

The type of ubiquitous, never-ending marketing of violence to children must stop. Violence is *not* child's play. We have enough public health research now to know the potential damage that can occur. What will it take to make these companies behave responsibly?

12

The Juvenile Literature Industry Is Marketing Violence to Children

Kathleen T. Isaacs

Kathleen T. Isaacs is a coordinator of sixth-grade and new-teacher programs at the Edmund Burke School in Washington, DC. There, she has taught humanities courses to sixth graders for over a decade. Isaacs is also a member of the American Library Association and has served on several prestigious awards committees that honor young adult literature.

Children's literature has always had its share of violent content, but recently the violence is becoming more explicit and grotesque: While in some cases, violence may serve a purpose in the narrative, more often the graphic images are either far too detailed or extraneous to the plot. Young readers commonly reject such graphic violence, preferring to avoid gruesome details or visceral episodes that are not a regular part of their own experiences. In fact, because real world violence is declining, hyping violent literature only makes readers believe that the world is more frightening than it is.

Sex and violence have been topics of YA books since the genre was invented. Realistically they can't be avoided. They are to a greater or lesser extent, part of teenage experience or their expectations of the adult world. But in YA

Kathleen T. Isaacs, "Reality Check: A Look at the Disturbing Growth of Violence in Books for Teens," *School Library Journal*, vol. 49, October 2003. Copyright © 2003 Reed Business Information. Reproduced from *School Library Journal*, a Cahners/R.R. Bowker publication, by permission.

publishing's early years, most of the action was offstage. When these topics first appeared onstage in single scenes, as in Robert Cornier's *The Chocolate War* (Pantheon, 1974) and Judy Blume's *Forever . . .* (Bradbury, 1975), they caused a furor. But now, 30 years later, we seem to be spared nothing. In particular, the amount of violence in books published for teens seems to be multiplying, and the descriptions include ever more disturbing detail. The same graphic explicitness that has been decried in films and [video] games increasingly turns up in young adult fiction and is endemic in the fantasy that so many young adults prefer. In my work with middle schoolers and as a longtime reviewer, I can't help but notice this troubling trend even in the best of the literature. In fact, reading hundreds of recommended titles for an American Library Association booklist called Best Books for Young Adults over the past two years has made me wonder where this violence, especially sexual violence, is coming from and what effect it might have on teen readers.

Are These Books Reflecting Young People's Real Lives?

Here are some examples from recent well-regarded books. In a scene in Kevin Brooks's *Lucas* (Scholastic, 2003), the protagonist is nearly raped by her brother's friends and the title character seems ready to cut the rapist's private parts with his knife. In the privileged world of Nick McDonell's *Twelve: A Novel* (Grove, 2002), the brother of a party-giver demonstrates his love of weaponry with a grotesque shoot-out. Even the cover appears as if it's spattered with blood. Is this casual violence a part of teens' lives that we don't see and doesn't get reported to authorities? In Dennis Foon's *Skud* (Groundwood, 2003), readers are shown four different ways of managing anger and violent impulses through the narratives of a brutal hockey player, a seemingly perfect air force cadet, a hardened criminal, and a boy who wants to play the role of punk. Is this how young men's lives are defined? Do we need to know all the gory details?

Child abuse, once carefully alluded to in stories of hostile, angry teenagers, is now exhaustively described. In E. R. Frank's *America* (Atheneum, 2002), Teresa Toten's *The Game* (Red Deer, 2001), and Jeanne Willis's *The Truth or Something: A Novel* (Holt, 2002), carefully sealed memories of sexual abuse leak out and overwhelm readers with vivid word pictures. In Adam Rapp's *33 Snowfish* (Candlewick, 2003) and Paul Fleischman's *Breakout* (Cricket/Marcato, 2003), the abuse is part of daily living.

The brutalities of detention centers are exposed in books like Jack Gantos's *Hole in My Life* (Farrar, 2002) and Rebecca Fjelland Davis's *Jake Riley: Irreparably Damaged* (HarperTempest, 2003). But do we need to see Jake abusing the calves? What is a reader to make of stories about the creation of a killer as in John Halliday's *Shooting Monarchs* (McElderry, 2003)? Do we need to know what it was like for three-year-old Macy to be tied to a swing in the rain?

A graphic novel like Steve Niles's *Thirty Days of Night* (IDW, 2003), which, in the text, is a rather ordinary vampire story, is liberally illustrated in page after page of blood spots. In a fantasy based on Icelandic mythology even more brutal than that of the Greeks, Melvin Burgess's *Bloodtide* (Tor, 2001) places readers right there as a character's legs are amputated.

While some [young readers] are enthralled [by book violence], many prefer not to read these books.

Readers Reject Violence

The middle school students I work with take sexual content in stride. They have been hearing about sex for years; they are familiar with the words even if they have not yet experienced the passions that lie behind them. Furthermore, this is information they want. They look forward to growing up to be sexual beings themselves. They can hardly wait.

Their reactions to explicit violence are quite different. While some are enthralled, many prefer not to read these books. Violence is pretty much absent in their own lives. Like the majority of young people today, the students I see do not live in a world where street violence is a regular occurrence, although they are quite aware that some of their age-mates do. They have never experienced corporal punishment in schools and many have parents who do not believe in spanking. They are surprised and concerned when a parent or teacher slaps, spanks, or beats a child in books we read together in class; such scenes inevitably provoke spirited classroom discussion. Actual physical fighting is a rare occurrence in their sheltered, supervised lives. During their primary-school years, they did not walk to school on their own and many have had relatively little unstructured play experience. They were not free to roam the neighborhood, whether their neighborhoods were city streets or suburban backyards and woods. Their understanding of violence comes from the screen and the printed page. They are both more familiar with the possibilities and less knowledgeable about actual pain and suffering. The comfortable cartoon world of characters that rebound from appalling disasters is certainly easier to take than a book that dwells on the feelings of a character suffering physical and emotional abuse. They don't much care for reading or hearing this.

Reading the details in a realistic novel is a very different experience from adding these from your own imagination. All readers re-create the text according to their own experience and understanding. In journals, a number of my students have noted that they prefer books that leave holes for them to fill with their own imagination. What are we doing to readers when we fill in the gaps, and particularly when we fill them with details of aggression and cruelty beyond the reach of their imaginations and experiences? Many readers are able to protect themselves [as, years ago, my fifth graders universally protected themselves by completely missing the rape in Jean Craighead George's *Julie of the Wolves* (HarperCollins, 1972)]. Could it be that we believe these young people, raised on pictures as well as words, are less able to make pictures in their heads? And are these the pictures they need? I do not believe that these gritty and raw books represent reality. I'm afraid that authors, editors, and book buyers in stores and libraries believe much of the hype they see in the media.

In the Real World Violence Is Declining

In truth, serious violent crime rates in the United States have declined steadily since 1993, and are now about half the level they averaged between 1973 and 1993, according to the Bureau of Justice Statistics. Homicide, rape, and robbery rates are way down. Across the United States, the proportion of serious violent crimes committed by juveniles has generally declined since 1993, as well. In Washington, DC, where I teach, the total number of juvenile arrests fell from 5151 in 1988 to 2102 in 2002. Two-thirds of those arrests are for what are called acts against property or acts against public order, rather than acts against people. While teens are most often the victims of violent crimes, that rate, too, has declined since 1993, from roughly 115 per 1000 to 55 per 1000. According to the National Clearinghouse on Child Abuse and Neglect, reports of child abuse have dropped over the past five years. In 28 U.S. states, corporal punishment is banned in schools, and there have been proposals for banning it in homes.

School shootings declined throughout the 1990s but stories of the conditions that might lead to such events like Ron Koertge's *The Brimstone Journals* (Candlewick, 2001), David Klass's *Home of the Braves* (Farrar, 2002), and Alex Flinn's *Breaking Point* (HarperCollins, 2002) continue to appear.

These well-written and thoughtful titles may be useful for discussing some of the underlying problems, but they do not represent the norm. How many of our schools are rife with seriously troubled, armed and dangerous youths? In 2000, 12- to 18-year-olds were twice as likely to be victims of serious violent crime away from school than when they were in school, according to the National Center for Education Statistics. The overwhelming majority of them were never victims of any sort. Between 1995 and 2001 the percentage of students who reported being victims of crime at school (mostly thefts) was down from 10 percent to 6 percent. But Americans seem to believe that these indexes are rising. In a 1999 NBC/*Wall Street Journal* poll, 71 percent of respondents thought a school shooting was likely in their community.

This belief has to arise from the extensive media coverage of juvenile crime. According to a study published by the Berkeley Media Studies Group and the Justice Policy Institute, "Although violent crime by youth in 1998 was at its lowest point in the 25-year history of the National Crime Victimization Survey, 62% of poll respondents felt that juvenile crime was on the increase." The authors of this study reminded readers that we all construct our visions of reality from what we have seen, heard, or read even more than from personal experience. If our news media plays up juvenile violence, as the 2001 study showed, we can't help but believe that this is what is going on in the world.

Neil Howe and William Strauss surveyed a large number of high school students and reported their findings in *Millennials Rising* (Vintage, 2000). They offer a much more hopeful vision of the newest generation of young adults. They described them as many things: optimists, rule followers, team oriented, sheltered, pressured, and achieving, but, in their words, "less violent, vulgar, and sexually charged than the pop culture being produced for them." This is certainly my own experience. This is not to deny that there are young people for whom such violence is a fact of life. They deserve the opportunity to see themselves in literature. Do they need the graphic detail? Will the rest of us be desensitized by our overexposure? Those of us who write for or select among and share books with young adults seem to be part of the problem when we emphasize violence. Can we be part of the solution?

Organizations to Contact

The editors have compiled the following list of organizations concerned with the issues debated in this book. The descriptions are derived from materials provided by the organizations. All have publications or information available for interested readers. The list was compiled on the date of publication of the present volume; the information provided here may change. Be aware that many organizations take several weeks or longer to respond to inquiries, so allow as much time as possible.

American Civil Liberties Union (ACLU)

125 Broad St., 18th Floor., New York, NY 10004-2400
(212) 549-2500
e-mail: aclu@aclu.org
Web site: www.aclu.org

The ACLU champions the rights set forth in the Declaration of Independence and the Constitution. It opposes the censoring of any form of speech, including media depictions of violence. The ACLU publishes several handbooks, project reports, civil liberties books, pamphlets, and public policy reports.

American Psychological Association (APA)

750 First St. NE, Washington, DC 20002-4242
(800) 374-2721
e-mail: public.affairs@apa.org
Web site: www.apa.org

The APA is a society of psychologists that aims to "advance psychology as a science, as a profession, and as a means of promoting human welfare." Although the APA believes that viewing television violence can have potential dangers for children, it opposes the creation of an age-based television ratings system. The APA produces numerous publications, including Children and Television Violence, and APA Denounces Proposed Age-Based Television Rating System.

Canadians Concerned About Violence in Entertainment (C-CAVE)
167 Glen Rd., Toronto, ON
  M4W 2W8
  Canada
e-mail: info@c-cave.com
Web site: www.c-cave.com

C-CAVE seeks to increase public awareness about the effects of entertainment violence on society. It serves as an educational resource center by collecting and making available information about violence in entertainment. C-CAVE promotes media literacy and responsible government and industry regulation of media violence as essential ways to achieve a safer, healthier environment. C-CAVE publishes various newsletters, reports, and brochures concerning entertainment violence.

Cato Institute
1000 Massachusetts Ave., NW, Washington, DC   20001-5403
(202) 842-0200 • fax: (202) 842-3490
e-mail: cato@cato.org
Web site: www.cato.org

The Cato Institute is a libertarian public policy research foundation dedicated to promoting limited government, individual political liberty, and free-market economics. It opposes government regulation of television violence and the installation of the V-chip. It publishes the quarterly *Regulation* magazine, the bimonthly *Cato Policy Report* and the periodic *Cato Journal*.

Center for Media Literacy
PO Box 64-1909, Los Angeles, CA   90064
(310) 581-0260 • fax (310) 581-0270
e-mail: cml@medialit.org
Web site: www.medialit.org

The Center for Media Literacy (CML), a nonprofit organization, provides educational materials that promote critical analysis of the media and its content. The organization's main goal is to empower individuals, from a young age, to make good decisions about their engagement with all forms of media. The group publishes a periodic newsletter *CML C*O*N*N*E*C*T*. The group also provides an online archive of the magazine *Media & Values* that was published from 1977 to 1993.

Entertainment Software Ratings Board (ESRB)
317 Madison Ave., 22nd Floor, New York, NY   10017
Web site: www.esrb.org

The ESRB is a self-regulating body for the entertainment software industry that rates video and computer games. The ratings are assigned so that consumers can make informed decisions about the games they are purchasing. The ratings are based on age-appropriateness and content. They provide guides for deciphering the ratings and have worked on public service announcements that help to clarify the rating system and its benefits.

Federal Communications Commission (FCC)
445 12th St. SW, Washington, DC   20554
(888) CallFCC (225-5322) • fax: (202) 418-0232
e-mail: fccinfo@fcc.gov
Web site: www.fcc.gov

The FCC is an independent government agency responsible for regulating telecommunications. It develops and implements policy concerning interstate and international communications by radio, television, wire, satellite, and cable. The FCC is required to review the educational programming efforts of the networks. It publishes various reports, updates, and reviews that can be accessed online at their Web site.

The Free Expression Policy Project (FEPP)
161 Avenue of the Americas, 12th Floor
New York, NY   10013
(212) 998-6733 • fax: (212) 995-4550
Web site: www.fepproject.org

The FEPP, part of the Democracy Program at the Brennan Center for Justice at NYU School of Law, offers information on free speech, copyright, and media democracy issues. Their research covers a broad range of issues including censorship and rating systems. They have published policy reports on these topics and fact sheets available online.

Media Coalition
275 Seventh Ave., Suite 1504, New York, NY   10003
(212) 587-4025 • fax: (212) 587-2436
e-mail: info@mediacoalition.org
Web site: www.mediacoalition.org

The Media Coalition champions the First Amendment right to free speech in all forms of media. It defends the American public's right to have access to the broadest possible range of opinion and entertainment, including works considered offensive or harmful due to their violent or sexually explicit nature. It opposes the government-mandated ratings system for television. Media Coalition distributes to its members regular reports outlining the activities of Congress, state legislatures, and the courts on issues related to the First Amendment.

National Cable & Telecommunications Association (NCTA)
1724 Massachusetts Ave. NW, Washington, DC   20036
(202) 775-3550
e-mail: webmaster@ncta.com
Web site: www.ncta.com

NCTA is the cable industry's major trade association. Its primary goal is to provide a single, unified voice on issues affecting the cable industry. NCTA works to advance the public policies of the cable television industry before Congress, the executive branch, the courts, and the American public. It publishes various reports and news releases that can be accessed at its Web site.

National Center for Children Exposed to Violence (NCCEV)
230 South Frontage Rd., PO Box 207900
New Haven, CT 06520-7900
(877) 496-2238 • fax: (203) 785-4608
e-mail: nccev@info.med.yale.edu
Web site: www.nccev.org

The NCCEV seeks to train individuals and raise awareness about violence, especially against children, in an attempt to reduce the occurrence of violent acts. They offer materials for parents and teachers that aid in the discussion about violence and include topics such as war, death, and disaster.

National PTA
541 N. Fairbanks Court, Suite 1300, Chicago, IL 60611-3690
(312) 670-6782
e-mail: info@pta.org
Web site: www.pta.org

The National PTA is the oldest and largest child advocacy organization in the United States. It opposed the original age-based television rating system and worked with the television industry and other child advocates to develop the age-plus-content-based rating system that went into effect in 1997. The National PTA produces *Our Children* magazine, various surveys, reports, and online bulletins on issues related to the health, welfare, and education of children and youth.

Parents Television Council (PTC)
707 Wilshire Blvd., #2075, Los Angeles, CA 90017
(800) 882-6868 • fax: (213) 629-9254
e-mail: Editor@parentstv.org
Web site: www.ParentsTV.org

The PTC was established as a special project of the Media Research Center. Its goal is to bring America's demand for values-driven television programming to the entertainment industry. The PTC produces an annual Family Guide to Prime Time Television, based on scientific monitoring and analysis gener-ated from the Media Research Center's computerized Media Tracking System. The Family Guide profiles every sitcom and drama on the major television networks and provides information on subject matter that is inappropriate for children. Various publications are available on the Web site including L. Brent Bozell's weekly syndicated column and current movie and television reviews.

TV-Turnoff Network
1200 29th St NW, Lower Level #1, Washington, DC   20007
(202) 333-9220 • fax: (202) 333-9221
e-mail: tvfa@essential.org
Web site: www.tvfa.org

TV-Turnoff Network, formerly TV-Free America, is a national nonprofit organization that encourages Americans to reduce the amount of television they watch in order to promote stronger families and communities. It sponsors the National TV-Turnoff Week, when more than 5 million people across the country go without television for seven days. It publishes the quarterly newsletter the TV-Free American.

Youth Free Expression Network (YFEN)
275 Seventh Ave., 15th Floor, New York, NY   10001
(212) 807-6222 ext. 22 • fax: (212) 807-6245
e-mail: ncac@ncac.org
Web site: www.ncac.org/YFEN

The YFEN is part of the National Coalition Against Censorship that opposes the censorship of information for young people and provides resources for adolescents to learn about their rights. The group also promotes the advancement of youth freedom of expression. They sponsor events to raise awareness about censorship, hold workshops offering alternative solutions to censorship at schools, and provide opportunities for young people to get involved in issues relating to censorship and free speech.

Bibliography

Books

Martin Barker and Julian Petley, eds. *Ill Effects: The Media/Violence Debate.* New York: Routledge, 1997.

Cynthia Carter *Violence and the Media.* Philadelphia: Open University Press, 2003.

Jib Fowles *The Case for Television Violence.* Thousand Oaks, CA: Sage, 1999.

Jonathan L. Freedman *Media Violence and Its Effect on Aggression: Assessing the Scientific Evidence.* Toronto, ON: University of Toronto Press, 2002.

Jeffrey Goldstein, ed. *Why We Watch: The Attractions of Violent Entertainment.* New York: Oxford University Press, 1998.

Dave Grossman *Stop Teaching Our Kids to Kill: A Call to Action Against TV, Movie and Video Game Violence.* New York: Crown, 1999.

Gerard Jones *Killing Monsters: Why Children Need Fantasy, Super Heroes and Make-believe Violence.* New York: Basic, 2002.

Douglas Kellner *Media Culture: Cultural Studies, Identity and Politics Between the Modern and the Postmodern.* New York: Routledge, 1995.

Steven J. Kirsh   *Children, Adolescents, and Media Violence: A Critical Look at the Research.* Thousand Oaks, CA: Sage, 2006.

Joshua Meyrowitz   *No Sense of Place: The Impact of Electronic Media on Social Behavior.* New York: Oxford University Press, 1985.

Neil Postman   *The Disappearance of Childhood.* New York: Vintage, 1994.

W. James Potter   *The 11 Myths of Media Violence.* Thousand Oaks, CA: Sage, 2002.

Harold Schechter   *Savage Pastimes: A Cultural History of Violent Entertainment.* New York: St. Martin's, 2005.

Karen Sternheimer   *It's Not the Media: The Truth about Pop Culture's Influence on Children.* Boulder, CO: Westview, 2003.

James P. Steyer   *The Other Parent: The Inside Story of the Media's Effect on Our Children.* New York: Atria, 2002.

Periodicals

David Edelstein   "Now Playing at Your Local Multiplex: Torture Porn," *New York Magazine*, February 6, 2006.

Lis Else and Mike Holderness   "Are the Kids Alright after All?" *New Scientist*, July 2, 2005.

Geraldine Fabrikant   "Need ESPN but Not MTV? Some Push for That Option," *New York Times*, May 31, 2004.

Charles Paul Freund	"Bhutan's Boob Tube," *Reason*, October 2004.
Katie Hafner	"Game Ratings: U Is for Unheeded," *New York Times*, December 16, 2004.
Anita Hamilton et al.	"Video Vigilantes," *Time*, January 10, 2005.
Bill Holland	"Industry Slow to Reform Marketing Violence to Kids," *Billboard*, May 5, 2001.
Brian D. Johnson	"Shades of Bloodshed," *Maclean's*, November 17, 2003.
Dan Kennedy	"The Daniel Pearl Video," *Nieman Reports*, Fall 2002.
Gina Kolata	"A Study Finds More Links between TV and Violence," *New York Times*, March 29, 2002.
John Leland and Peter Marks	"A New Look for Entertainment in a Terror-Conscious World," *New York Times*, September 24, 2001.
Samantha Mille et al.	"G-Rated Revolutionary," *People*, February 17, 2003.
National Catholic Reporter	"Firms Profit by Editing the Dirty Bits Out of Movies," September 9, 2005.
Nature	"A Calm View of Video Violence," July 24, 2003.

Lola Ogunnaike and Jeff Leeds — "An Arbiter of Hip-Hop Finds Itself as the Target," *New York Times*, March 16, 2005.

Ann Oldenburg — "Ratings System Runs Adrift," *USA Today*, July 28, 2005.

Megan Othersen Gorman and Sari Harrar — "Violent TV Makes Kids Violent Adults," *Prevention*, September 2003.

Joseph Pereira — "Games Get More Explicit—And So Do Warning Labels," *Wall Street Journal*, September 25, 2003.

Richard Rhodes — "The Media-Violence Myth," *Rolling Stone*, November 23, 2000.

Joe Saltzman — "Why Can't You Say—Or Show—That on TV?" *USA Today Magazine*, May 2004.

A.O. Scott — "True Horror: When Movie Violence Is Random," *New York Times*, March 23, 2003.

Todd Shields — "Violence as Indecency," *MediaWeek*, June 7, 2004.

Cheri W. Sparks and Glenn Sparks — "Why Do Hollywood and TV Keep Showing Us Violence," *USA Today Magazine*, January 2001.

Karen Springen — "What's On When You're Snacking?" *Newsweek*, December 13, 2004.

USA Today Magazine — "Video Violence Desensitizes Brain," April 2006.

Cynthia G. Wagner "Aggression and Violent Media," *Futurist*, July/August 2004.

Juliette H. Walma van der Molen "Violence and Suffering in Television News: Toward a Broader Conception of Harmful Television Content for Children," *Pediatrics*, June 2004.

Sharon Waxman "Study Finds Film Ratings Are Growing More Lenient," *New York Times*, July 14, 2004.

Karen Wright "Works in Progress," *Discover*, April 2003.

Index